THE NEW G MENTALITY

Investing in your development, not your demise.

2nd Edition

THOMAS C. COTTON III

THE NEW "G" MENTALITY – Investing in your development, not your demise.

TABLE OF CONTENTS

PREFACE

Gang members and their associates have been engaged in a war of survival and relentless challenges throughout their lives, which have defined their lives. The severe environmental and economic hardships due to systemic neglect often led them to find ways to make quick money and develop strong bonds of brotherhood with others in the same struggle. As they are navigating a complex and often treacherous environment, they are seeking identity, respect, and security, which requires taking risks and making tough decisions.

Most communities in which street gangs exist are deeply affected by structural inequities that have persisted over generations and are influenced by social determinants of health. Through economic struggles, lack of educational opportunities, and limited access to vital resources, an environment is shaped where individuals see gang involvement as their only possible option to improve their lives, despite the harmful consequences.

Because the stories and truths of gang life are unquestionably tough, I request that you approach the content and possibilities with an open mind, reading through the lens of empathy and understanding. The goal is not to glorify or condemn gangs but to highlight the many factors that lead individuals to join gangs and to explore new opportunities for change. With this perspective, efforts can be made to address root causes and break ongoing cycles of violence and instability.

The New G Mentality serves as a rallying cry to encourage policymakers, community leaders, educators, and society at large to collaborate in addressing gang issues. However, the greatest appeal lies in encouraging gang members to step up, recognize their collective power, and take the initiative to make the change they want to see.

Everyone is encouraged to recognize that punitive measures are not the answer, and change requires an urgent need for comprehensive new strategies. As you read through this book, you will encounter opportunities to champion investments in people through education, economic opportunities, business ventures, and community programs aimed at redeveloping gang areas, reducing violence, and improving communities.

Uniting for justice and fostering reconciliation presents an opportunity to sustain positive change and establish improved pathways toward a more promising future for individuals affected by social determinants of health.

Taking the time to understand challenges should inspire us and broaden our perspective, enabling us to identify and develop sustainable, effective solutions. As these solutions are created, seeds of change are planted that grow over time into a more just and compassionate society where everyone has the opportunity to flourish and live free from environmental harm. Making this a reality shifts the current narrative and paves the way for a brighter future. The power for a movement is within our reach, and the hope is that the New G Mentality will be one of the sparks that guides our actions.

ACKNOWLEDGMENT

I dedicate this book to those who have been caught up in the gang lifestyle or environment and lost their lives or freedom to incarceration or death. These lives illustrate the reality of structural violence.

May we never forget the individuals who lost their lives tragically. The memories and untold stories of each name, each face, each story that was cut short are the heartbeat of this movement. I extend my deepest sympathies to the families and communities affected by loss and tragedy.

May we also never forget the devastating toll of incarceration and the greater impact it has. I will never forget the moment I engaged in a conversation with an individual who told me he had been sentenced to double life plus forty years for selling drugs. This person isn't alone. Numerous others have received lengthy sentences and life imprisonment due to their involvement in the drug trade.

Every strategy written, every program launched, and every system challenged carries your legacy forward. May this work stand as a living memorial that not only remembers but actively redeems, ensuring that future generations inherit safer streets, stronger families, and communities where life is valued and dreams have room to grow. Your absence is a constant reminder that transformation is not optional; it is urgent.

To advocates, activists, scholars, and everyone dedicated to empowering an often overlooked community and dismantling unjust systems while building new pathways for growth, thank you for your unwavering dedication. Many of you are deeply engaged in this effort, and I would like to take a moment in this book to recognize your contributions. This is an invitation for all to join you on this vital journey. Let's continue to collaborate and foster progress, supporting the mission of transformation.

Thank you to every reader who picks up this book. My hope is that you walk away with at least three commitments to make a difference in the New G Movement or understand how you can address the roots of structural violence. When each of us contributes even a small effort, the collective effort will help us achieve big goals. May this book inspire awareness and drive the movement forward.

INTRODUCTION

The New "G" Mentality is a fresh mindset that believes those with lived experience can develop themselves if they have access to new opportunities and become the leaders to steer street culture toward purpose and progress. It recognizes that traditional approaches to dismantling gangs have failed because they overlook the strengths within gangs, including discipline, loyalty, and leadership. Instead of focusing on dismantling the existing structure, the New "G" Mentality serves as a guide to redevelop the organizations by empowering the people who carry both the scars and strength of the streets to become leaders of change.

For those who have not been involved with gangs, the New "G" Mentality is rooted in giving grace to people who are seeking better lives and have tried to make that happen with the options available to them. The focus is not on what's wrong but on finding ways to further opportunities for people in these environments to elevate themselves without taking major risks.

People often overlook that gang members face daily traumatic challenges and still continue to work to survive. Despite their work often involving illegal or harmful activities, they show up daily and literally put their blood, sweat, and tears into surviving. The lack of other opportunities strengthens their dedication to their lifestyle, building bonds that encompass love, loyalty, respect, power, and family.

This sense of belonging reaches a level where they feel responsible for the people they are committed to fighting alongside. Together, they strive to push back against oppressive forces and death at every turn. Because they don't have to face the challenges alone, their shared hope and deep desire to "make it", whatever "make it" means to each individual, can truly inspire and uplift everyone around them as their shared hope and deep desire grow. This connection fuels the courage that drives the grit and determination to overcome any obstacle in the way or die trying.

Although it may not be immediately apparent, the grit and determination exhibited by gangs are similar to those of individuals who wake up daily to work in unfulfilling jobs or those driven to start a business. The main difference lies not in their work ethic or effort but in the opportunities available to them, which are shaped by their starting point in life.

What some call a "criminal enterprise" can also be understood as a form of entrepreneurship born out of necessity, involving the organization of people, risk management, product movement, and logistical problem-solving; skills that are transferable when the environment offers a lawful path. Redevelopment, then, is about harnessing that same grit and relentless drive to build businesses, lead civic efforts, and break cycles of poverty. It reframes the gangsta persona from a mask for survival into a mantle of leadership, showing that the strength once used to endure the struggle can now be used to transform the struggle itself.

The gangsta persona is more than just an image. It is a testament to survival, resilience, and power in the face of seemingly impossible odds. It is often a response to systemic scarcity and exclusion, which becomes an armor forged by fire. Behind the tough exterior and street bravado, there's a reality shaped by struggle and determination. In this world, loyalty is currency, and trust is earned through actions, not words.

This lifestyle adheres to distinct street codes and demonstrates allegiance to their respective crews. It creates an allure that promotes the hope of overcoming societal, neighborhood, and personal struggles. It tells a story of a pathway to success, but does not highlight the other side, where many do not succeed.

My involvement with gangs started at a young age, when I was around Crip and Mexican gangs. As I got older, I stayed cool with my Mexican friends but started gravitating to my family and friends who were Crips. In my city, like in many cities back then, the Crips outnumbered the Bloods, but that didn't matter because there were more issues and conflicts beyond just the two gangs. There was Crip-on-Crip violence, other gangs around town, and the random people who just wanted respect or to take what you had, and all types of mess that kept me always lookin' over my shoulder. Since we weren't far from LA, gang bangin' was all around me.

During my teen years, I found myself getting deeper into the lifestyle. Even though I was in it, I didn't have a deep understanding of other gangs because of my lack of exposure. I just knew I was loyal to those who were loyal to me, and that was all that mattered.

As I branched out to other cities, both within and outside California, my knowledge began to broaden with my different experiences. I encountered various sets of Crips and Bloods, Mexican gangs, as well as a lot of gangs I had never heard of before. All of them were similar, but never the same. The similarities revolved around the strengths of discipline, loyalty, and leadership.

When I went to prison, my learning went to the next level. I was schooled about the history of many gangs in California, as well as gangs from the Midwest, South, East Coast, and other places. Listening to different OGs share their stories about their beginnings and the people before them was truly a lesson in street knowledge. What stuck out to me the most was the many commonalities across their experiences, regardless of their geographic background.

One story that has always stood out to me was the many people who shared the stories about the beginning of the Crip and Blood main rivalry, which started in the early 1970s and grew from there. From its small beginning, the gangs gained momentum to the point where there are hundreds of Crip and Blood gangs across America. To think, a movement was built off small groups of people who disagreed and took sides, and the rest is history.

This story is significant because, at the time of this writing, we are looking at approximately fifty years of gangs doing the same activities without creating the change needed for their communities. Instead, we are experiencing skyrocketing rates of incarceration and death, combined with poverty that has a chokehold in most gang neighborhoods, which creates a significant challenge to find hope and the ability to do something different.

The policies, laws, structural inequities, social determinants of health, and other challenges that impact underserved communities where gangs are located have kept these areas relatively unchanged. As a result, generations of gang members continue to cycle through, unaware of how it all started, but they adopt the lifestyle and perpetuate the same chaos, with the hope that it will make a difference. They are only following the script of fighting to survive against overwhelming odds and the environmental challenges of daily life.

It's understandable when people are struggling to find the most effective way to overcome major challenges, they will sometimes do whatever is necessary and available to them. I have engaged with thousands of people who were sold out to the gang lifestyle due to their environmental and personal struggles being severe, persistent, and not just isolated incidents. Their daily challenges compelled them to seek a viable path forward and strive to make new ways for their lives.

Having access and exposure to gangs became their main option for fighting through the daily challenges. The lifestyle was attractive because it offered several opportunities for change. However, the outcomes were not favorable, but that didn't matter because it was an all-in lifestyle.

Through most of my interactions with gang members and my personal experiences, it is known that there is an internal conflict within most because the lifestyle can be taxing. I cannot say this is true of all gang members, as my knowledge and access to everyone is limited, so I can't fully understand every gang member's experience. However, those I have interacted with make it clear that they share the same common feelings about the challenges of the lifestyle.

I have personally asked over fifteen thousand people if they would choose to be in a bad situation and face hardships, and every single person expressed some form of the word 'no'. On the flip side, all fifteen thousand people answered 'Yes' when asked if they wanted a better life. Many of these people were involved with gangs and/or had been incarcerated. I invite you now to consider these questions yourself, and your answers will likely be the same.

Although people in gangs are deeply involved in the lifestyle, many still believe that death and destruction aren't what life is all about, and there must be more. From this, we should be able to see that the desire for a better life is inside all of us, but the way we chase that better life can be the problem. Sadly, systemic barriers and limited exposure restrict opportunities in underserved communities to pursue a different way for a better life, forcing people to use whatever access they have to get ahead. Up to this point, that's all they know. The good news is, even though that's all they know, it isn't all they have to know.

This book is about sparking a movement that creates new opportunities for change by helping gangs redevelop their infrastructure to empower their communities. It aims to prevent the senseless loss of loved ones to violence that can be avoided, support community members, and break cycles that have produced ongoing hardships.

I won't explore the complexities of how people join gangs and their affiliations, as the many differences in gang structure make generalizations difficult and potentially inaccurate. I also won't categorize what makes a person a gangsta or an "OG". The focus is on the shared mindset that goes beyond being a part of a gang.

Some individuals have genuine gang ties, while others do not, but that doesn't make them more or less of a gang member. The main factor is whether someone is committed and actively involved in typical gang activities or is associated with a crew that engages in similar activities. To outsiders or to the criminal justice system, such individuals would be seen as gang-affiliated. Therefore, for this book, whether you are genuinely connected to a gang or just affiliated, you'll be regarded as having a G mentality.

This approach makes sense because, even if a person hasn't officially joined a gang, they still participate in behaviors associated with a broader gang culture. Their actions reflect gang traits, and the communities that produce these outcomes are connected to them. People with this mindset usually do what is necessary to survive in their environment.

This is a space where the hardships and challenges collide, becoming the battlefield of the daily war to survive. To an outsider, it isn't viewed as war, even though the communities have been described as war zones. However, for those who are in the trenches, it is a daily battle in a war. Those who are in the same trenches are the ones who understand this toll and its impact on a person, both physically and mentally. The sad part is that they usually cannot see the full impact until they are out of the war zone.

This inability to recognize the harm done in the war zone is similar to that of military personnel who go into combat and face hardships. Often, the true impact on them only becomes clear once they leave the war zone and return home. Likewise, police officers who endure the physical, emotional, mental stresses, and trauma of their job often remain unnoticed until they are away from duty. The key point is that all these individuals do what is necessary to survive and succeed; yet the lack of support for managing stress allows personal harm to go unchecked, taking a toll on them in many ways.

We must remember that at the core, people are simply people. No matter the uniform they wear, the neighborhood they live in, or the label society gives them. Everyone responds to pain, pressure, and the need for survival in similar ways. The harshness of life often drives people to build protective walls and coping mechanisms just to get through the chaos. When we take the time to understand why people do what they do and humanize their choices, whether in soldiers, officers, or young people on the streets, we can begin to see that these responses are not about good versus bad, but about survival. And it is from this same place of survival that gangs in America have their roots.

Gangs in America have existed for decades, with some lasting over a century, so we know they aren't going anywhere. Historically, many efforts to dismantle or disband them have consistently failed. One of the main reasons is that it is difficult to tear someone away from their family, with whom they are deeply connected. So connected that they are willing to die for one another.

We can draw on years of experience and research to recognize that persistent gang activity negatively impacts the community and its members. A common strategy used to improve public safety has been to work towards breaking up gangs. On the surface, this approach seems reasonable. However, this line of reasoning fails because it ignores what has been built: family, loyalty, protection, and identity. I won't even attempt to explore how the chemical connections, such as dopamine, influence experiences in the lifestyle, but that's part of why the lifestyle's appeal is so powerful.

Dismantling gangs is like trying to erase someone's identity because it's taking away their protection, connection, and family. Gangs go deeper than most people realize, and members will fight hard to maintain their way of life. This is why most members find it difficult to leave their gang.

The harsh and unfortunate reality for many gang members is that, despite their dedication and loyalty, their lives often do not get better. In fact, in many cases, their situations get worse. The very things that bond them to the gang, like protection, identity, and family, are often torn apart through violence, incarceration, and death. Communities suffer from poverty and other environmental determinants of health that have a negative effect because of gang activities. This is not a judgment of individuals or communities, but rather an observation that something different needs to happen. It also highlights the fact that the connection is strong and meaningful to those involved.

Therefore, the best way for people, families, and communities to improve is for gang culture to improve. Redeveloping the existing infrastructure and teaching everyone to empower others will uplift the families and communities to which they belong. People in gangs play a significant role in this, as well as in personal safety and growth, which are among the main benefits of the New G Movement.

Gang networks operate much like legitimate social networks despite having different goals and outcomes. Their structure includes job opportunities, hierarchies, divisions of labor, communication channels that support their activities, and competition. Just like in the corporate world, members of these networks specialize in roles such as distribution, enforcement, or recruitment. However, the nature of their products and the consequences of their actions set them apart. Instead of providing goods or services to help their community, gang activities often lead to violence, exploitation, and social harm.

If we compare the street economy with legitimate corporations, it highlights deep societal disparities and systemic problems. While both involve strategic planning, market competition, and profit motives, their results differ greatly. Legitimate businesses operate within legal boundaries, meet consumer needs, and create wealth. In contrast, the products of the street economy often involve illegal activities that drive further criminal actions, affecting communities with violence, dependence, and destabilization. This underscores broader societal issues and systemic challenges. What cannot be overlooked, though, is that it also shows **there is not a workforce gap**, but rather a lack of access to products and development that leads to better opportunities.

This is where an opportunity for a seismic change can happen. If individuals within gang networks had access to new ventures, access to business capital, and corporate strategies, they would likely seize these new economic opportunities. This access would support job growth and other workforce opportunities, enabling people to utilize their talents and thrive without fear of harm.

For this to happen, the root causes of the disparities require comprehensive solutions that go beyond simply highlighting criminal activity. They must address socioeconomic inequities, offer viable alternatives, and create pathways for gang members to unite and succeed without resorting to illegal means.

To support the new pathways, the New G Mentality elevates individuals to take personal responsibility in breaking the cycle of poverty, incarceration, and death. By strengthening the G's higher-order thinking skills, they become stable leaders who intentionally uplift their communities and create opportunities for growth, rather than contributing to their demise. This growth results in enhanced living standards, enabling them to act as catalysts for creating opportunities that elevate the quality of life for others.

People involved in gangs are often seeking to improve their lives. Economic disparities create such desperation that individuals become indifferent to their own fate. Remember, the desire for a better life is in all of us. Therefore, most people find their way to a better life through the methods they are most familiar with and have been exposed to. For gangs, the environment in which they grow up influences their personality, systems, hierarchy, identity, and many other aspects.

The beauty of their lifestyle lies in being part of a structured system and a family-oriented environment where keeping their family safe is a top priority. Proposing the redevelopment of gang areas is a way to address this issue by keeping family structures intact, while providing alternative options for wealth, health, and community.

Dismantling the gang structure is not the answer; instead, it's about offering new options. When they have alternatives, they can join a system that encourages growth and development, helping them invest in a brighter, more positive future.

Many people only know what they've been taught to survive, and those involved in gang life tend to repeat these patterns. History demonstrates that with this mindset, real change remains elusive, and the same cycles continue to repeat themselves. It is essential to understand that relying on others to establish fairness may never occur. Proactively taking action is crucial to achieving the fairness you deserve.

The hope is to see gangs learn to use their infrastructure to develop their people, create opportunities for positive change, and support their communities, rather than continuing to suffer the loss of loved ones. The goal is to break negative cycles related to violence and incarceration and to live up to your potential by setting higher standards, ultimately leading to better outcomes for everyone.

It's time for the G's to take action and become the change they want to see. The New G Mentality is vital for the movement to transform lives and create the better futures everyone seeks. For meaningful change to occur, it must originate within the community and include gang members, who will serve as the primary catalysts for these positive changes. They need to adopt the mindset that this will not be a quick and easy fix, but rather they must be willing to dedicate the same fifty years that it took for gang culture to develop in California, although it will not take fifty years to see significant change.

When opportunities and options become more accessible to gang members, it will significantly solve major societal problems. However, creating lasting change demands efforts beyond those of the gang members alone. It requires people from different backgrounds and experiences to come together and align systems to achieve better outcomes. By collectively embodying this movement, G's are empowered to become the leaders they were meant to be and pursue a higher purpose.

Chapter 1

Good Trouble Mentality: Igniting Justice and Inspiring Change

The New G Mentality aims to empower gang members who have been involved in self-destructive behavior and offers them a blueprint for their redevelopment. When I started writing this book, I immediately thought of 'Good Trouble'. While the term 'Good Trouble' may initially appear to be an oxymoron, its true meaning depends on the nature of the trouble involved. If the trouble results in difficulties, problems, disorder, or distress that ultimately have adverse outcomes, then it cannot be considered good. However, the late Congressional Representative John Lewis, who popularized the phrase 'Good Trouble,' stated, "... if you see something that is not right, not fair, not just, do something. We cannot afford to be quiet." If that is you, then you might be actively creating 'Good Trouble' to stand up for justice, equality, and equity.

Growing up in California, I was only familiar with the "popular" civil rights movement leaders, such as Dr. Martin Luther King Jr. and Rev. Jessie Jackson. However, after moving to Atlanta, I became more aware of many other leaders dedicated to civil rights causes. Congressman John Lewis was one of the key figures I learned about, and he stood out because he was still alive and active in the Atlanta communities. He dedicated his life to racial justice and equality, embodying this commitment until his passing in 2020.

He began his journey toward equality as a young man, and by the age of twenty-three, he had already established himself as one of the key leaders of the civil rights movement. In one of his speeches, he said, *"Do not get lost in a sea of despair. Be hopeful, be optimistic. Our struggle is not the struggle of a day, a week, a month, or a year. It is the struggle of a lifetime. Never, ever be afraid to make some noise and get in **Good Trouble**, necessary trouble."*

During the August 28, 1963, March on Washington, Lewis spoke passionately about the injustices of that era. Many of the issues he highlighted back then are still with us today, just in different forms. During his speech, he stated, "Let us not forget that we are involved in a serious social revolution." This served as a rallying cry encouraging people to participate in creating change. A shift was necessary for effective civil rights laws because no government party was acting in the interests of the oppressed. His main message was to motivate people to recognize the injustices they were currently facing and to take action to address them.

The New G Mentality isn't about backing politics or pledging allegiance to a party; it's bigger than that. This is a call to action to rise with the Good Trouble Mentality and see this movement through until the end.

We are surrounded by a sea of challenges and injustice, yet the same old methods continue to recycle broken systems and produce the same broken results. The New G Mentality refuses to play that game. It is not about temporary fixes or expecting politicians to fulfill promises they cannot keep. Instead, it emphasizes building from the inside out, reclaiming our power, and transforming past destruction into a guiding force for progress. This movement aims to restore dignity, unlock leadership potential, and harness our collective unity for unstoppable change.

While the call to develop a Good Trouble Mentality is powerful, we cannot lose sight of the truth that most people are just trying to survive day to day, the best way they know how. Survival mode is a heavy place that creates tension, often leading people to bend the rules of life, where anything goes just to make it through.

For the people outside of these experiences, it may seem simple to say, "do something different," but the weight of structural barriers and cultural norms can prevent people from even realizing that change is possible. The problem isn't that they don't want to do something different. It has to do with the lack of access to the ways and means to turn that desire into reality. This gap creates a vortex that pulls people back into the same cycles again and again. The New G Mentality refuses to ignore this reality and encourages us to break the vortex, to humanize the struggle, and to build real pathways where survival can finally give way to transformation.

In gangs, the current acceptable types of trouble don't safeguard the well-being of the people around them or their communities, no matter how much the gang members love both deeply. Many people aspire to improvement, but they often resort to questionable means, hoping to eventually do what is right, even if it first means doing what is wrong. Having this mindset leads to harm for many, as only a few will succeed in overcoming obstacles. Even those who do make it through carry wounds, scars, or trauma. For the rest who don't make it, issues like death, poverty, and incarceration are their reality.

To create real change, we must understand that getting into 'Good Trouble' is not just an idea, but a core piece of a new lifestyle. It is a progressive movement rooted in protecting the people you love. It challenges us to think critically about what we must shift individually, so we can collectively open wider doors of opportunity. At its heart, it is the recognition that the greatest resource in any community is its people. When we empower one another, we don't just create for ourselves, but we create for the collective good, lifting individuals, strengthening families, and transforming entire communities.

Too often, the storyline is that people in gangs or from underserved communities cannot work together to build anything good. Even though there are many cases where this hasn't been true, the dog-eat-dog world is the narrative that hinders collaboration and collective efforts to overcome hardships and adversity. The common narrative often suggests that people in gangs or from underserved communities are unable to collaborate effectively and work to build something good.

It is unfortunate that people within gangs see life from a competitive and aggressive perspective, rather than focusing on collaboration and development to overcome challenges and hardships.

One reason this narrative is popular and a shift to collaboration has not taken root is that many communities have lacked access to effective training and resources on how to overcome barriers, build better systems, and create sustainable pathways for long-term growth. Without the development tools, the future is often sacrificed to the present's urgency.

When immediate needs go unmet, long-term alternative solutions lose their appeal, no matter how good they sound. The desire for change remains, but when money is tight and survival is at stake, people do what they must to get through the day. That's the reality, but it doesn't have to be their destiny.

For the most part, gang members currently work and build together, so it isn't far-fetched that people in gangs and from underserved communities can come together to develop new ways to meet daily needs. If it weren't for the element of danger or the threat of prison, many of the illegal enterprises would be major successes because of their work ethic, the intangibles they possess, and the dedication to meeting the outcomes, even to the point of losing their lives.

Redeveloping the framework of gangs and learning to create positive changes can greatly influence the lives and surroundings of families and communities. When gang members enhance their critical thinking and creativity while being supported by new methods to adopt their New G Mentality, they can develop more effective ways and means to create positive economic engines that overcome financial obstacles.

Building on 'Good Trouble' can serve as the catalyst to unite and develop innovative strategies that unlock opportunities for entrepreneurship, employment, growth, investment, and other possibilities an open mind can imagine. This strategy offers hope to those who have been negatively impacted by their environment and are making difficult decisions about the direction of their lives. It creates a path that provides an alternative for them to rebuild their lives safely and legally. It is an opportunity for the gang family to truly unify and focus on their development, avoiding actions that jeopardize their safety or freedom. This serves as the beginning of a journey toward a new, purposeful life.

For those who wish to continue believing that illegal activities are more profitable than legitimate solutions to financial challenges, there are two key points to consider. First, you need to commit to living a new way of life for the long term before you can honestly judge if illegal activities are more profitable. Only by committing to something new and dedicating years of effort can one determine if a new lifestyle is more profitable or not.

Second, you must take time to think about whether the profit gained through illegal means is worth the time spent in prison, away from family, friends, and the sacrifice of your freedom and future. Additionally, is it worth the price of losing the life of someone close to you to pointless violence? It is also certain that money cannot remedy the persistent cycles of chaos and trauma associated with these experiences.

Creating a Good Trouble Mentality involves looking beyond everyday distractions to identify opportunities for making a positive impact. It means rising above excuses that keep you stuck and taking responsibility for the justice and equality you desire. Embracing the New G Mentality acknowledges that this type of growth cannot happen in isolation. It will require a community of people working together to support one another and find solutions to overcome challenges.

Trying something new is challenging because of past experiences and current lifestyle, which makes it easier to find reasons or excuses that keep you stuck. Since you only know what you currently know, it is crucial to actively seek new information and connect with people who can guide you toward different knowledge and opportunities for a better life. As you become an innovator in shaping your new world, you will gain access to resources that enable you to make a difference and become a trailblazer in creating justice, equality, and freedom.

A trailblazer is someone who is the first to do something new or innovative. They forge a new path, enduring bumps and bruises to create a trail that others can follow. Trailblazers embrace the Good Trouble Mentality by understanding that their efforts to make a difference are greater than themselves. They understand that their fight lasts for days, weeks, months, and years. It is a lifelong commitment to ensure future generations have better opportunities, a space to develop their lives, and the motivation to engage in some 'Good Trouble,' necessary trouble.

Those who show unwavering commitment to creating progress are often not recognized or celebrated at the start of their journey. But what if people in gangs, rivals, and underserved communities adopted the Good Trouble Mentality to address and transform their communities at the same time? This wouldn't be such a lonely road, and it might feel easier to overcome the present circumstances and pursue new aspirations.

Instead of being willing to die for each other, they begin to demonstrate deep loyalty, dedication, and a willingness to live for one another. Rather than risking their lives for their cause, they focus on investing in the well-being of future generations. By attaching their same unwavering commitment and loyalty to the New G Mentality, a movement will accomplish the promise that genuine transformation will happen. The amazing part is that many trailblazers would be involved in forging new pathways, and the movement would be bolstered and expanded through a committed effort to improve things and build a better world.

If you have ever felt dissatisfaction from witnessing injustice, personal hardship, or seen the struggle of others, then the fire for change already burns within you. It stems from the awareness that something is wrong and that your world can and should be different, even as you walk through and see the same cycles of life daily. This discontent within you serves as fuel for the changes you wish to achieve.

When you reflect deeply on your true desires, beliefs, and actions, you will continue to ignite the spark that sets the transformation in motion. Reflection awakens you to see your world differently and lays the foundation for reconnecting to your true values. The true test is having the faith to act on what you see and trust that something better will emerge, even as you face life's challenges.

This is why adopting the Good Trouble Mentality is essential to your new lifestyle. The principles empower you to succeed beyond your current circumstances through consistent, positive actions. It challenges your existing thinking and systems that uphold the current norms. It encourages you to push boundaries and shake things up, while embracing the New G Mentality lifestyle of not abandoning your family, gangs, or community, but instead working to create positive change. As you change yourself, you are also intentional in creating a legacy and transforming the lives of others for the good of future generations. One that creates a culture of development, not demise.

Stepping into your new purpose requires you to work just as hard, if not harder, than you did for the streets to make room for meaningful change. As I mentioned earlier, this work leads you to a place where you're willing to live for each other rather than die from one another. The seeds of discontent planted in your life will continue to act as the spark that drives you toward your new lifestyle. Your new principles will be the catalyst that inspires those around you to come together and take action despite the opposition ahead.

To be honest, this is a hard road, but you also must recognize that the old road is hard too. This is where the New G Mentality requires you to decide which hard path to take. You can opt for the path that you are currently on, which preserves the current way of life with all the associated risks, or you can switch to the one that fosters safety, freedom, and a legacy for your children, community, and future generations. The choice is yours; **choose your hard.**

For some, this vision may sound inspiring but impossible. For others, it may stir uneasiness, as if stepping into change means betraying who you are or selling out on your people. These feelings are real, but they are also part of the process. Change will always come with challenges, especially when you've lived a certain way for so long. Shifting direction will feel like going against the grain, but understand this: it is not about quitting on yourself or your people. It is about growth that leads to the development of your full potential.

When you have the New G Mentality, you channel the same loyalty, love, and energy you have always carried and make it a constructive force. Just as you created a pathway in the gang for destructive behaviors, you are now forging a pathway for your people to transition from destruction to the development of opportunities that bring life. It is about caring for yourself, your brothers, sisters, their families, children, and community.

The dedication that fueled the streets can be redirected to build skills, talents, and resources to fight injustice. This mobilizes those around you, turning survival into leadership and passion into a movement for justice, opportunity, equality, and human rights. This isn't about leaving your people behind; it's about leading them forward.

When you begin to develop empathy and compassion for others, it is not about being soft. Thinking of others is a stronger choice than being self-centered, because you have decided to start a journey to build something for others, even if you may not see the end result. As you overcome your own struggles and challenges, you choose to **live a legacy** that overcomes destruction and demise.

The journey to adopting the Good Trouble Mentality is not without tests. Common challenges include opposition from established interests, criticism from society and peers, systemic barriers, and personal sacrifices. Personal trauma and deep internal conflicts can also try to hold you back. Nevertheless, as you remain dedicated to this path, stay determined and find strength in your convictions, as well as the support of like-minded individuals who surround you. Over time, you become the leader of building a legacy of positive change. Your actions will create a ripple effect, reaching beyond your immediate circle and inspire others to join the movement for a better world.

The New G Mentality is a journey from doing wrong to a transformative and empowering process. The Good Trouble Mentality involves a shift in perspective, a commitment to disrupt harmful norms, and a relentless pursuit of positive change. Those who adopt this mentality embody empathy, courage, resilience, and grit, demonstrating that even in the face of adversity, one person can make a significant impact on the world by choosing the path toward redemption. Survival may have guided your history, but the New G Mentality shapes your future.

Real Stories 1: Finding My Way...

I believed that the hardness of the streets was my only classroom, shaping my understanding of loyalty, survival, and respect. However, loyalty and survival brought a lot of pressure, making me feel like I was dying a slow death.

I still had respect for the ones I was loyal to, so when I first started making changes, I wasn't sure I would be able to do it. I was skeptical of others and wasn't sure how it would work. The thought of doing something different gave me hope, but I had to figure out how to deal with real life, like making enough money for rent, probation, and how I was going to provide for my family.

What really helped me was seeing brothers like me making different choices. I began with small steps, like reading, taking classes to improve myself, and accepting jobs I previously thought were "beneath me." These small actions helped me grow. It is a different type of hustle, so I have to stay on top of it. Struggles remain, but I feel free in my mind, and that's a victory.

Chapter 2
Growth Mentality: Unlocking Your Potential

The Growth Mentality is the belief that you have the ability, power, and right to expand, improve, and raise the standards of your life, no matter what your age, or regardless of where you have started from. In the context of the New G Mentality, it means maturing to a point where you refuse to be confined to a single story about your life, whether shaped by the streets, systems that label you, or the limits others place on your life.

Growth isn't about perfection but rather progress toward seeing challenges as obstacles to overcome, setbacks as setups for elevation, and each day as a new chance to build something better. More than just personal success, it multiplies possibilities for your family and community, pushing you to outgrow destructive patterns, unlearn survival-only thinking, and channel your resilience, creativity, and leadership toward building a lasting legacy, rather than following cycles of devastation.

People with street knowledge have already demonstrated a Growth Mentality by learning to adapt and function within their environment, which itself is a distinctive growth journey. Using limited options to survive and handle risky or tough situations has sharpened survival skills. However, these skills are usually not applied in places with the greatest growth potential. So, what usually happens is that once people in gangs have learned a way to survive, there is little effort given to learn new ways of living. There has to be more opportunities than just survival and risky behaviors if change is going to happen. Other opportunities must be presented that are interesting enough to reignite their Growth Mentality in individuals, enabling them to want to learn and reach new levels beyond their current knowledge and rebuild their collective.

Facing immense hardships and challenges in life causes fatigue, frustration, impatience, and even trauma. These feelings can make it harder to maintain a positive Growth Mentality. While it's natural for most people to want to overcome life's barriers and have new experiences, finding the path to new opportunities can sometimes be difficult and out of reach.

Many gang members come from adverse situations, but they have learned ways to support themselves and become street savvy. Unfortunately, what they have built is fragile and not sustainable. It is only a matter of time before what they achieved in the streets falls apart in some way or another. With every setback, the pressure is heightened, and the determination to be successful increases because it feels like death is looming. With the increased pressure, the illicit activities intensify, and it becomes a matter of time before one of the consequences, such as incarceration, being robbed (jacked), or even worse, death, crosses their path.

The environments in which people grow up typically determine the opportunities they have and influence the choices they make throughout their lives. This is also shaped by who is willing to teach them how to survive and how easily they can access that teaching. By being around the hood, the lessons are often not spoken but learned by watching and copying what happens. However, there are times when street knowledge is actively passed on.

The ability to get this knowledge is essential because it offers a means to survive. However, if the learner took a broader view of what is required for this knowledge and its outcomes, they would realize that this is a short-term survival strategy, not sustainable for life. Nevertheless, choosing to live the gang lifestyle is a decision that many accept, and it requires dedication, loyalty, a strong work ethic, and a willingness to learn and adapt. Learning gang activities isn't something people are born with, nor is it a lifestyle they naturally seek. It is something picked up along the way, because it seems like the only way.

Through this, we can see that this is a learned behavior, not a natural one. No one is born seeking destruction or chaos. Those patterns are taught, absorbed, and reinforced by environment, trauma, and survival needs. This realization should bring hope because it means transformation is possible. If destructive cycles can be taught and normalized, then the New G Mentality, which fosters new cycles of growth, peace, and purpose, can also be taught and normalized as well. We can rewrite life's lessons, reframe the definitions of power and success, and model a different way of living that still honors strength but channels it toward growth and development instead of demise. This is the heart of redevelopment: helping people unlearn what harms them and equipping them to learn what heals them, so that entire communities can embrace a new rhythm of life where thriving becomes the standard rather than the exception.

This is where empathy transforms into strength. Moving beyond judging the choices and learning to understand the reasons behind them, we open the door to connecting with the people who are often dismissed. Every decision holds a story, and recognizing the survival instinct behind each choice is a beginning point for transformation. When different worlds come together and collaborate, innovative growth solutions will arise.

Through this foundational principle of the New G Mentality, the same grit, discipline, and resilience that once fueled survival in the streets can now be leveraged to build businesses, raise families, and lead communities.

Just because we are taking an empathetic approach doesn't excuse destruction; it merely redirects it for constructive purposes. This process is not about condoning the harm caused by gangs, nor is it about erasing their struggle and origins. It is about resetting and redeveloping gangs to prove that our next steps can change everything for generations to come. If they were sharp enough to learn the game, they could be strong enough to change it.

Through my many conversations with individuals involved in gangs, I have heard many say they wish there were other clear, accessible opportunities for building a different future, because they more than likely would have chosen those paths. Those have been some powerful statements to hear. The significant challenge is that without clear and accessible opportunities, immediate needs often take priority, making it difficult to commit to a different way forward.

Creating new opportunities that meet urgent needs and inspire hope is crucial for reducing desperation and encouraging positive change. This development has the potential to instill hope and promote a Growth Mentality, motivating individuals to make healthier decisions, realize their potential, and strive for a better future.

It is impossible to precisely determine all the immediate needs or what might cause someone to feel desperate; however, by utilizing research on the many social determinants of health (SDOH) or Maslow's hierarchy of needs, we can begin to gain a better understanding of these factors. It is well-researched and documented that areas where gangs thrive are impacted by many SDOH.

According to the U.S. Centers for Disease Control and Prevention, the definition of SDOH is "non-medical factors that affect health outcomes. They include the conditions in which people are born, grow, work, live, and age. SDOH also includes the broader forces and systems that shape everyday life conditions." So, to ask a person who has many environmental SDOH factors to pull themselves up by their bootstraps is not a fair assessment of the trials they must overcome.

Regardless of what you think of the lifestyle gang members choose, SDOH leads to many Adverse Childhood Experiences (ACEs), which are real, and survival becomes their default mindset. Therefore, in addition to addressing these SDOH, there needs to be options for better choices, allowing people to transition from surviving to thriving.

People involved in gangs and those who have never experienced that lifestyle must develop a Growth Mentality to understand that surviving and thriving can coexist. However, if a person focuses only on survival and not success, no matter how many steps they take toward achieving success, they will remain trapped in a scarcity mindset. This is evident because people are willing to risk everything, seeking ways to survive and escape their lack.

When people, especially young people, are exposed daily to illegal options for making money, sometimes involving substantial amounts, they often see a way to care for their needs and more, which makes it difficult for them to become interested in a safer and more promising legal path. The risk of an illegal lifestyle is accepted because the reward seems worth it. Mix that with desperation and a lack of skills, and it is easy to see how a person can choose to be all in for the streets. The downside is that even when it seems worthwhile, the return is rooted in more suffering. It is fun in the beginning, but pain in the end.

To get people to see alternative ways to overcome their situation requires creating a movement and making a genuine effort to support transformation. For some, it could be a matter of showing them a different way, and they can adapt and take it from there. For others, there are different SDOH that must be overcome, such as literacy challenges, health access, food insecurities, violence, trauma, and many other things. Ultimately, helping them through their process involves taking the time to understand their current situation, listening to establish trust, and creating a structure that supports their development.

By listening, trust and understanding are developed. It's not about focusing on ways we believe will help their situation. It is about making space to learn from those who are going through challenges because the main goal is to elevate the individual and support transformation. It is about gaining an understanding of the crucial factors that have driven them to a point where they live risky lives and see no way out due to numerous barriers.

Previous efforts to change gangs have focused on encouraging members to leave their gangs to change their lives or attempting to dismantle gangs altogether. While this approach may have seemed like the only way, it has generally proven ineffective. This approach does not create a dignified way of recognizing that all people have something to offer.

Gang members often desire new opportunities; however, their deep dedication to their lifestyle and connection to their gang family make it difficult for them to consider alternatives. This bond often prevents them from exploring options outside the gang, limiting their ability to pursue a better future. Their attachment is deep because for most, it is the only life they've known. Their mindset is all about protecting their lifestyle, which hinders the Growth Mentality and prevents a possible shift in life.

By welcoming gang members to lead in creating new opportunities to redevelop the gang, it addresses the connection between gang members, their needs, and the protection of their families. It creates a dignified way to improve lives and care for the community, while building toward a better future.

If you are outside the gang lifestyle, but understand the challenges that people affiliated with gangs face, as well as the potential for change, you have a role to play. Embracing a Growth Mentality goes beyond believing change is possible. It involves deliberately looking past the surface issues and engaging in the work of developing solutions. Communities affected by gangs cannot rely only on those with lived experience for their transformation. It also depends on outside individuals who are willing to invest their time, resources, and influence in creating new opportunities.

This support does not equate to pity or charity; rather, it signifies collaborative partnerships. It recognizes the strengths, resilience, and leadership inherent in individuals within gangs and helps guide these qualities toward constructive, life-affirming paths.

The Growth Mentality recognizes that genuine change occurs when entire communities come together in upward progress. Such progress relies on the contributions of business leaders, educators, faith communities, policymakers, and ordinary citizens who choose not to turn away but instead dedicate themselves to creating opportunities for others.

When individuals outside of gangs embrace this mindset, they become active participants in driving change rather than mere observers. They foster an environment that supports a shift from survival-driven choices to those focused on purpose, entrepreneurship, family stability, and community healing. Thus, the Growth Mentality transcends personal growth; it represents a shared responsibility that fortifies sustainable transformation.

For programs to make a meaningful and lasting impact, they should be designed intentionally and backed by a genuine commitment to growth. Superficial outcomes, such as those achieved solely to justify ongoing funding, may produce short-term results, but they do little to create lasting change. An effective approach requires a long-term investment in human development and an understanding that transformation is not a single event but a continuous process.

Generational harm cannot be reversed with quick fixes. Instead, it demands decades of ongoing empowerment, based on the idea that healing and growth should happen throughout a person's life. Programs should not target just one stage of life but be designed to work with kids in their childhood, support them during adolescence, prepare them as young adults, and continue to assist them as parents, workers, and leaders. This lifecycle approach ensures that change is continuous and reinforced at every critical stage of human development.

Furthermore, individuals who have undergone transformation should be reengaged to contribute to the future design and implementation of programs. Their involvement not only confirms their growth but also enhances the overall impact, thanks to their unique ability to mentor, instruct, and uplift others. This process fosters a generative cycle in which transformed individuals serve as agents of community renewal, thereby expanding the fidelity of programs, as well as the scope and depth of empowerment.

The goal isn't just about fixing old systems, but about constructing entirely new ways that focus on purpose, opportunity, and caring for everyone. It is building a culture where positive change spreads far and wide, where one person's transformation inspires not just another person, but entire communities. The Growth Mentality becomes more than just an idea. It becomes a practical and inspiring approach to driving significant, system-wide, and community-wide improvements.

The Growth Mentality encourages community members, government agencies, and faith organizations to focus on people, because that is what truly matters for change. Systems need to move beyond merely mentioning individuals in programming, statistics, and research data to a point where they are recognized as subject matter experts and are viewed as individuals with valuable real-life experiences.

Programs and agencies tend to gather evidence of the problems they aim to address, but they often lack tangible or sustainable solutions to make it a reality. Once the program ends, community members are left to navigate their next steps on their own. To improve programming, for every issue identified through statistics, a corresponding solution should exist if we are willing to commit to the long-term advancement of society.

Within the Growth Mentality, statistics alone cannot serve as the sole indicator of an evidence base. Listening to the voices of individuals involved in gangs and those from under-resourced communities is crucial in guiding the development of resources. I am not suggesting the elimination of existing programs, because some support is better than none. Still, we need a broader approach that emphasizes long-term solutions and sustained support.

Recognizing gangs as a resource and valuing their members as community assets rather than threats encourages exploring ways to empower and strengthen these systems from the inside. This approach does not ignore the negative history associated with gangs. Instead, by learning their stories and addressing the social determinants of health (SDOH), we can foster a Growth Mentality that unlocks new potential for community development, helping to keep everyone safe.

Another challenge is the capacity to elevate critical thinking and foster the construction of bridges rather than fostering division. Throughout my lifetime, numerous narratives and perspectives have arisen regarding whether individuals who commit crimes or belong to gangs should be helped, often based on the harm they have caused. However, these perspectives seldom account for the historical devastation inflicted upon marginalized communities. If we just go back to the 1960s, a range of policies, laws, and processes have contributed to the destruction of communities. Regardless of personal opinions or narratives, whether valid or not, the systemic issues resulting from these measures persist in communities today.

To develop real solutions, we must go beyond making excuses for failing to tackle the interconnected challenges of gangs, poverty, and social determinants of health. What's needed is a Growth Mentality mindset that views problems not as permanent barriers but as chances to create new pathways forward. Instead of confining people to silos that perpetuate generational harm, doors must be opened up to healing, innovation, and progress. It begins with exposing people to new experiences, healing past wounds, and committing to personal growth as the foundation for achieving higher levels of transformation.

Within gangs, accountability is crucial for maintaining their traditions and codes. Although the street code may not be the most effective way to progress, it is deeply ingrained as a way of life. Raising the Growth Mentality and accountability within these groups involves everyone being responsible for training peers and ensuring they learn all necessary steps to pursue new opportunities. This approach isn't fundamentally different from previous methods. It simply repurposes the same efforts for positive outcomes. Everyone must still take ownership of their personal roles and be supportive of the growth of others.

Let's look at an example of how this process can work. A gang member is arrested and enters the juvenile justice system. Once in this system, they have the chance to engage in positive change. They take responsibility for starting programs that teach them how to avoid harmful activities and build a solid foundation for a better future. During this period of transformation, their peers, family, and street support group can also be included and offered similar programs, forming a cohesive group from the inside out. As this group continues with the programs, they create a stronger, more supportive network for the individual who is incarcerated. They also begin to work on preventing further arrests because they are building something meaningful.

The key connection here is that the person in the system genuinely wants to protect their support group and community from harm and incarceration. In turn, their support group and community hope that this person will be protected and have new opportunities upon release.

Typically, when a person comes home from incarceration, their immediate needs hit fast. They step back into a community, often their gang family, that offers instant belonging, even if it pulls them in the wrong direction. Even after taking advantage of programs that helped them grow, they often return to a support group that didn't have the same opportunity to learn or heal.

The moment they feel the familiar embrace of loyalty and support, whether it's from someone giving them cash, drugs to sell, or simply celebrating that they are home, it can undo progress and pull them back into the same cycle that led to their incarceration. That gap creates a dangerous disconnect, where the progress made behind the walls is quickly overwhelmed by the pressure of survival.

This is the difference with the New G Mentality. While the person was incarcerated, their community support systems were also being equipped with the tools and training to grow alongside them. So, instead of reentering the same environment that once pulled them back, they would come home to a circle already prepared to support and reinforce their change. Their circle can provide another level of love and support, which is essential for ongoing change, reducing the fear of reoffending, and helping them avoid activities that could hinder their progress.

This shift could transform reentry from a return to old cycles into a launch pad for healing, growth, and lasting success, benefiting not just the individual but also laying a stronger foundation for the entire community.

Through this process, people gain real access to jobs and entrepreneurship, building the skills to succeed as employees or business owners while developing the confidence to lead change. As a core element within the New G Mentality, individuals are empowered to take ownership of their actions and influence those around them. Just as important, it strengthens their circle of peers and relatives on the outside, creating a culture of accountability and shared growth. Together, they can break destructive cycles and replace them with new outcomes that uplift not only themselves but also their families, communities, and the broader society.

This example illustrates how individuals can overcome past mistakes and decisions. They start to build hope and work toward a future without fear of leaving others behind. When everyone starts to take responsibility for their decisions and life direction, they discover new opportunities that previously didn't exist. They begin to lead the necessary changes themselves. This hope is a foundation for lasting transformation.

This growth enables individuals to remain resilient and adaptable by learning from their past actions, gaining strength from experiences, and using them as stepping stones rather than stumbling blocks. People will develop the courage to turn setbacks into opportunities while maintaining a strong determination to overcome any new challenges.

Individuals committed to cultivating a Growth Mentality actively seek opportunities to learn and develop new skills. They apply these skills to drive change and foster positive connections. This mindset, combined with increased education and access to new systems, boosts hope and serves as a gateway to empowerment, opening doors to better opportunities, safety, and a brighter future, while broadening their outlook on life.

The Growth Mentality is pivotal to transformative coaching and mentorship. Regardless of what we think about gang culture, there's no denying that coaching and mentorship take place within the gang. The idea of learning from the big homie or the OG is a tradition that has been handed down for years. The OG has always done their best to pass on what they know. Even with their limitations, they mentored with what they had. As the OG's knowledge grows, they share that wisdom with those coming behind them. This is transformative coaching and mentorship.

This interaction is not formal but relational and develops organically. Young individuals are eager to learn and, therefore, seek out individuals willing to provide guidance through life's complexities. Let us not overlook that they also assist them in financial matters. Among these leaders, a charisma exists that attracts followers.

The appeal of The New G lies in the same core attributes as the previous G, now complemented by new knowledge that can be conveyed to peers and younger generations via the same relational engagement. The New G offers new methods to direct individuals toward healthier lifestyles and constructive decision-making. They are building upon the foundation of coaching and mentoring to foster growth and enhance community well-being.

This Growth Mentality is a deliberate way to pay it forward and take responsibility for uplifting communities and keeping people safe. Because others desire personal growth, they are drawn to the New G, hoping to learn how to start their own journey toward a better future. By sharing their stories and supporting others, they create a ripple effect that reaches well beyond their own lives. The peak of the Growth Mentality occurs when transformed individuals become agents of positive change, actively participating in community initiatives, advocating for resources, and working toward creating a more equitable and vibrant environment for everyone.

Ultimately, those who accept the responsibility of being the New G will live a legacy to ensure they pass on a legacy of empowerment. It becomes a testament to the resilient human spirit, showcasing the incredible capacity for transformation when the right support, perspective, and opportunities are combined with determination, accountability, and a thirst for knowledge. The stories of success will become beacons of hope, illuminating the path from the streets to empowerment for generations to come.

The journey to overcome personal and environmental battles is not an easy walk. It stands as a testament to growth, dignity, and the power of collective effort in creating the necessary changes for better life outcomes. There must be clear and supportive guidance on how to help people unlock their full potential. Areas of study such as technology, business, trades, finance, spiritual development, and many other fields will help people find hope in a different system of success.

The process doesn't end there. It requires individuals equipped with resources and capabilities to support the New G lifestyle and turn ideas into reality. A Growth Mentality recognizes that merely talking about solutions isn't enough; it demands long-term investments in implementation to ensure sustainability. Since the development of gangs didn't happen overnight, investing with a future-focused mindset and long-term committed resources is necessary to establish a lasting legacy.

Building hope must embody the potential for change inherent in all of us. By combining the right opportunities, mindset, and support with the determination and resilience already within individuals, anyone can rise above their circumstances with the New G Mentality.

Real Stories 2: Looking Back at the Old Me

I look back at my old self, and it's almost like watching a movie of someone else's life. I see a young man chasing a reputation that never paid him back, losing time to the system, losing friends to bullets, losing family to disappointment. But I also see myself grinding, showing me that my drive wasn't broken; it was just misdirected.

Still, when I look deeper, I see something else. I see a hunger that would not quit and a determination that kept me moving even when I did not understand where I was going. My drive was never broken. I was just pointed in the wrong direction. I had discipline and the courage to take risks, but I wasn't doing the right things.

Once I started slowing down, I began to understand the same focus that once fueled me held the power to build me into something better.

Now, instead of trying to prove how hard I am, I prove I can build. When I look back, the pain built the platform for my purpose and now fuels my business.

Chapter 3
Grit Mentality: Ten Toes Down; Mindset Up

The Merriam-Webster dictionary defines grit as a "firmness of mind or spirit: unyielding courage in the face of hardship or danger." The Grit Mentality is the relentless determination to persist regardless of obstacles, setbacks, or pain.

Within the New G Mentality, grit represents the endurance essential for transformation. It involves a refusal to quit when faced with adversity, along with the discipline to keep learning and implementing your new life plan. Grit is the force that once fueled you to push through the struggle, but now powers the rebuild.

Grit is something you are already familiar with because it's the same drive and toughness that pushed you through chaos. When life turned cold, it was the resilience that kept you standing when the odds were stacked against you. It was the determination that shaped you through the struggle when nothing came easy.

As your life begins to shift, you will need to harness your raw willpower, elevate it, and redirect it toward building businesses, protecting families, pursuing education, and creating opportunities that break destructive cycles.

The Grit Mentality calls you to be Ten Toes Down, Mindset Up. Ten toes down means standing firm in loyalty, authenticity, resilience, and accountability, rooted in your values and committed no matter the pressure you face. Mindset up means refusing to be limited in your thinking, choosing instead to rise with vision, strategy, and purpose. Together, they represent the posture of someone anchored by grit but guided by growth; unshakable in foundation, yet constantly lifting their perspective toward higher ground.

Embracing and making your transformation through cultivating a new mindset will be challenging. It requires you to question your current habits and beliefs while remaining open to new and unfamiliar changes. Remember that the path you're following now is hard, and you've experienced its negative effects, either firsthand or through someone you know. Since both building a new life and maintaining your current way of living are hard, the decision of which difficult path to choose is yours. So, I will remind you one more time, **CHOOSE YOUR HARD**. Keep in mind, you're capable of going down either road, because you've developed the grit and determination to be successful both ways.

Grit is built by facing life challenges head-on. Instead of passively accepting obstacles like poverty, you work hard to overcome them, despite resistance, turning nothing into opportunities for survival. You have endured devastating experiences that would stop most people, but your grit allowed you to take life's punches and keep striving for something greater.

The New G Mentality doesn't develop simply because you desire change or take steps to improve your life. It requires grit, meaning a steady, committed, and disciplined effort to implement the necessary changes to become the person you aspire to be. It is a shift in mentality and lifestyle that involves clarifying your vision of a better life, enabling you to look beyond problems and understand that **each and every issue in life has a solution**.

Elevating your Grit Mentality involves committing to long-term self-improvement while finding healthy solutions to tough problems in your life, family, and community. When you first developed your Grit Mentality, it was shaped by the knowledge and experiences available to you. When you faced major challenges, you worked through them to the best of your ability. Through grit, you learned to push forward at all costs, even risking your life; you were dedicated to your process.

As you cultivate the New G Mentality, you'll need to consistently draw on that grit again and again. This time, instead of dedicating yourself to things that lead to your demise, focus on your development to live a better life. You must be willing and committed to push yourself hard to reach the next level, understanding that this doesn't guarantee immediate improvements in your life. It simply means you are dedicated to building your future and won't give up when life pushes back.

In personal growth, Grit Mentality drives determination, resilience, and a commitment to change. It motivates you to overcome distractions, rewrite your story, and create a future driven by the possibilities that come from your strong resolve, because you believe the new outcomes are worth it.

The Grit Mentality is often instinctive for people involved in gangs; it is deep-rooted within them. They take considerable risks in their daily grind that could lead to prison or death, all in pursuit of a better life. This grit is also necessary to overcome the mental health challenges and traumas of growing up in the hood or losing loved ones to incarceration or violence.

Constantly trying to find ways to get through life's devastation without losing all hope should be recognized, not looked down upon. The many ways the Grit Mentality manifests in people fighting to do what's necessary to make a conscious decision to pursue change are a strength that should be fostered, not destroyed. Unfortunately, this strength is often not seen as a valuable resource but instead used to perpetuate the cycles of trauma.

The persistent side of grit can also have a negative side that can be used to oppress others, especially toward those facing similar struggles. When trying to get ahead, many people inadvertently hold others back without realizing that everyday words and rejection can be particularly harmful, especially for those with low self-esteem.

Grit is powerful, but it can also be misapplied or misdirected, allowing it to be weaponized. For example, when a child gets good grades, peers in some settings might mock them for being smart, saying things like, "You think you're better than us because you're smart," or bullying them for being book-smart instead of tough. Over time, the child may shift their focus away from growth and excellence, lowering their own standards just to fit in. In these moments, peers are showing grit, but it's grit aimed at pulling others down rather than lifting everyone up. This kind of misguided determination can create a cycle where grit doesn't uplift the group but traps them in mediocrity or harm.

Grit should not be misused to harm others just because of differences. This fosters hopelessness in future generations and hinders efforts to overcome systemic barriers. Instead, channel your determination towards ending the unnecessary violence for yourself and others facing similar challenges. This shift demands a new perspective, recognizing that the true enemies are systemic forces, not your neighbors involved in gangs.

By blending your Growth and Grit Mentalities, you can intentionally work towards transformation and healing for yourself and those around you, even when the odds seem tough. This approach will help you ignite positive change and inspire some Good Trouble. Over time, it becomes clear that embracing discomfort as part of the ongoing journey is essential for growth. You'll begin to genuinely celebrate the successes of others and collaborate to create better opportunities, instead of viewing those around you as expendable for personal gain.

The remarkable thing is you only have to be intentional about redirecting your existing Grit Mentality toward fighting for the greater good. Instead of directing this energy toward criminal acts or just surviving, channel it into building successful businesses, earning degrees, and reaching high-level positions.

You might recognize that previous efforts to improve your community haven't always been enough. This realization underscores the opportunity to make a difference in the exciting journey you're about to embark on, driven by your desire to make things better. Whatever change you're aiming for, remember that having the discipline to follow through is key to staying dedicated to your growth. The bright future you envision is within reach when you adopt a broader vision of transformation that extends beyond your current circumstances. So, be ready to invest your time and determination, because turning your dreams into reality is worth every effort.

Grit Mentality thrives in a reservoir of resilience, but it must be fueled by hope. This hope is unbreakable, grounded in the faith that your efforts have meaning and will not be in vain. It comes from the belief that your path will lead to better results than your current options. Your commitment to the movement highlights the importance of trusting and embracing the process of change for everyone.

As your vision and purpose become clearer, you realize that overcoming barriers is part of your growth journey. Embracing the Grit Mentality allows you to face ongoing challenges and stay determined to reshape your life's direction. You will remain committed and not quit prematurely, allowing success and growth to manifest. You become stronger and transform fears into faith and obstacles into opportunities for advancement. With a more defined vision and purpose, you will create positive ripples of change. Your story will motivate others by showing how grit can shape their future, reframe their life narratives, and pursue meaningful change.

At each stage of growth, draw from your personal experiences and new knowledge to develop your New G Mentality. Use these moments to recalibrate your critical thinking to find more sustainable solutions. When facing failures or hurdles, lean into the Grit Mentality and rely on your faith to push you forward. Then use your innovation to proceed with renewed energy.

The Grit Mentality embodies dedication to transformation and growth. It fuels your drive to push beyond your current limits and relentlessly pursue progress that can reverberate through communities and future generations.

Real Stories 3: In the Middle of Struggle

I'm not at the finish line yet. Truth is, some days it still feels like I'm just stepping off the starting block. The race isn't easy. I still fight with my old ways and don't want to take the responsibility to make my life different. When my money is low, the pressure builds up, sometimes the streets start calling, offering that familiar escape I know too well. But now there's another voice inside me that is steady, grounded, and wiser. It cuts through the noise and reminds me not to waste what I have been given.

I have the chance to mentor young ones in my neighborhood. I see them light up when I take the time to listen, and it reminds me why I keep going. Their hope reflects my own progress. I've learned that giving back isn't something you wait to do after you've "made it." It starts right in the middle of the climb, when you're still building, still learning, still figuring it out. That's when your lessons are freshest and real. Giving while growing keeps me humble, focused, and accountable.

I know we can do better. I see what's possible when we rise above what used to hold us back. I understand that if I want others to believe that change is real, I have to keep pushin' forward. I want to be an example, so the work starts with me, for them. I know it is in us, and I want to show it's possible.

Chapter 4

Grateful Mentality: Learning to Let Gratitude Lead You Higher

Before you start reading this chapter, for the next 30 seconds, take this moment to pause and reflect on five things you are grateful for at this time.

The Grateful Mentality encourages us to recognize blessings even during difficult times and to value every small step forward. Gratitude isn't about ignoring pain or pretending life is easy, but about gently guiding our minds to be thankful for what we have instead of focusing on what we lack. It neutralizes bitterness and unlocks breakthrough.

A Grateful Mentality is crucial for the New G because it changes the atmosphere around you. Practicing gratitude helps you stay grounded under pressure, value those who support you, and build resilience by recognizing that progress is possible. It shifts your perspective from mere survival to genuine appreciation, transforming bitterness into hope and entitlement into humility. Gratitude acts as a lens that shows opportunities instead of obstacles, allowing you to see potential where others see only barriers.

The essence of the Grateful Mentality is in making the most of what you already have. By appreciating your existing resources, talents, and relationships, you create opportunities for greater creativity, vision, and growth. Gratitude forms the foundation of legacy because, by valuing today, you lay the groundwork for a stronger tomorrow.

Finding things to be grateful for can be difficult, but doing so might even save your life. The New G is someone who recovers from life's reckless moments and learns to see many reasons to be thankful. They then take their gratitude and use it as motivation to elevate their life.

When you struggle to feel grateful, it's usually because your focus is on what you lack, how you compare yourself to others, or lingering resentment from the past. These thought patterns can block your ability to see the blessings already present in your life. During those moments, remind yourself that simply having the chance to grow and improve is a gift in itself. You can also reflect on times when your life could have ended but didn't and let the memory of surviving stir a deeper sense of gratitude.

When life is good, it's easy to notice many things that make you feel grateful. However, during tough times, your view of what to be grateful for can become unclear or taken for granted. Learning to be content and to appreciate simple things is a healthy first step toward developing a Grateful Mentality. Contentment is a state of satisfaction or fulfillment with your current life situation, even during difficult times. It encompasses a sense of peace, acceptance, and gratitude in the present moment, without dwelling on what you lack.

Contentment differs from complacency or a lack of ambition. It involves appreciating your life and opportunities while also acknowledging your desires for growth and progress. Essentially, it can be summarized as: "Just be thankful for what you got."

Finding joy and fulfillment in simple things helps you feel comfortable with your life without constantly needing external validation or material possessions. If you constantly seek approval from others to feel worthy, you will often receive less recognition than you deserve. Your true worth is much greater than what you own or can acquire.

As you practice gratitude and recognize your contributions to others, you begin to affirm your worth and realize there is still much untapped potential within you. This mindset motivates you to see and develop your abilities, even when others do not recognize what you possess.

People who knew you before your transformation might still remember your former G mentality and often compare you to your past self. We all face limited perspectives at times, so there's no need to dismiss those who don't recognize your progress and potential. However, they shouldn't have a voice in validating or convincing you to turn back. If you allow this, you're letting them steal your vision, grit, growth, and gratitude, which can prevent you from getting into some Good Trouble.

Just like all the steps you take to grow in your New G Mentality, coming from the streets with a Grateful Mentality isn't easy. You may have experienced many hurts, losses, and traumas, and the process of healing and overcoming these challenges can be difficult. Changing your perspective is a step that can foster gratitude and support you on your healing journey.

An illustration of changing your perspective to support your healing journey is when you experience the loss of a loved one. It can evoke feelings of deep despair and hurt, which are entirely natural and valid. However, within each loss, there is often a moment where changing how you see things can lead to feelings of gratitude and growth.

The loss of a loved one is regularly expressed through sorrow and the thought of never being able to have them nearby again. It can also be rooted in grief and guilt. Whatever emotion is felt, it is genuine, and it is a testament to how that person truly added value to your life. You are expressing the emotion that best fits you. However, another suitable emotion is gratitude.

Choosing gratitude for these moments allows you to shift your perspective and see the many good experiences, as well as express the positive impact they had on you. Being grateful that you had the chance to know this person can transform pain into strength and propel you toward healing.

Just know that grief and gratitude are not mutually exclusive; they are rooted in the same underlying value: a deep connection to the person in your life. Both emotions can be expressed, validating the complexity of your feelings. However, there is still an opportunity for gratitude in every situation.

Coming from the streets, choosing gratitude and embracing the New G Mentality can evoke a complex range of emotions. As you begin to change, you may wrestle with guilt because you now have opportunities that others around you may not have. Rather than allowing guilt to weigh you down, shift your view and see this as an honor. Dedicate your growth to those who could not make it this far, carrying their memory with you as fuel for your progress. By transforming guilt into purpose, you not only honor them but also give meaning to your transformation. This perspective gives a different level of motivation to keep moving forward, stay committed to your change, and inspire others who are watching your journey.

Gratefulness is a way to lessen the impact of hurt, loss, and trauma, but it doesn't erase memories. Guilt won't rewrite their story; it will only weigh you down. When those feelings try to pull you back, remind yourself that your growth is a shield for others. Every step forward creates new opportunities to protect, to teach, and to break cycles that once trapped your circle. Let it ignite your drive, power your discipline, and remind you why you can't stop now. Every obstacle becomes proof that you're moving in the right direction, every step forward becomes a victory for those who couldn't take it, and every win becomes a light for others to follow.

Expanding your mindset means training yourself to see life from higher angles, shifting your perspective, and developing a Grateful Mentality that keeps you moving with purpose.

Another reason you might struggle to feel grateful is when you reflect on past experiences, you'll recall the many people and events that caused you pain. Often, the people who caused the harm were simply trying to survive, and you got caught in their own chaos. Even though they were trying to find ways to escape their daily struggles and trauma, their reckless actions still affected you negatively. Some were so hurtful that you can't see a way to move past them. Forgiveness will be essential here.

Forgiveness can be challenging because it often requires confronting the pain associated with specific events. While there might be reasons to hold onto resentment and anger, doing so only harms you because the other person has moved on.

Learning empathy and shifting your understanding of the person who harmed you is a way for you to let go and be released from carrying the burdens of hurt that are weighing you down. Sometimes empathy and understanding are gained when you examine your own actions to understand how you may have caused harm to others. Yes, moving forward from the hurt inflicted by others can start by looking inward at the hurt you have caused.

By understanding what drove you to deceive and harm others and how far you were misguided, you can gain clarity on why the people in your life could have been misguided to act the way they did. This reflection can also evoke remorse for what you have done, even if you believed it was right at the time.

The understanding gained helps you gain clarity on how and why people might have hurt you. You may start to notice that those who caused you hurt also faced their own struggles and pain, which shaped their behavior, just as yours did. You were all affected by different challenges and poor decisions that shaped your responses, which then caused harm to others.

This understanding is crucial because it gives you a foundation for living with a forgiving heart toward others, freeing you from the mindset that has hindered growth and gratitude. It's essential to acknowledge that while understanding and forgiveness are valuable, **they do not excuse what happened to you or your actions**. Instead, they offer freedom from being stuck in the past and help you learn to move forward.

At this stage, you can choose to hold on to the old things and risk further harm or let go of them and transform that energy into motivation. Taking responsibility over your past enables you to process every thought, feeling, frustration, and emotion, then combine them with gratitude and channel that power to move forward toward your new life goals.

Learning to forgive yourself for harmful and difficult decisions you've made is something that shouldn't be overlooked. The empathy you show others should also be directed inward toward you. Aim to reach a point where negative thoughts no longer dominate your self-perception, as **your inner voice is the most influential voice you will hear.** No matter what others can say about you, it doesn't compare to what you say about yourself to yourself. Show yourself some grace and understanding.

I want to emphasize an important point about forgiveness. **Forgiving others and yourself for harm doesn't mean excusing the harm that was caused.** When others acted in ways that led to pain, and when you made choices that led to harming others, these were real events that caused others to experience hurt that cannot be excused away. However, forgiveness allows you to release the hold these hurtful experiences have over you. It enables you to see your world differently and free yourself from the anchor that tied you to a moment in life that has weighed you down. It transforms anger and pain into healing and growth. Remember, forgiveness is ultimately for your benefit, not theirs, as it supports your healing process.

Practicing gratitude daily is a powerful tool for healing wounds caused by life, family, and the street experiences. Your personal journey fosters greater empathy, enabling you to understand how others feel when facing challenging situations. This awareness allows you to see others as flawed humans, just like yourself, rather than as the negative labels your mind might assign.

It's evident that life's struggles influence how people on the streets make survival choices, and they are not your enemies. Demonstrating empathy and understanding builds connections with those around you, turning everyone into a symbol of hope and healing.

When gratitude guides your actions, you honor both your past and the legacy you are building. You recognize that the opportunity to live a new life may seem impossible, given all you've endured; yet, every day is a gift meant to be lived for your development and shared for your growth. This mindset reflects the Grateful Mentality, inspiring resilience and perseverance. You continually seek ways to grow and enhance your life, valuing every opportunity, no matter how minor.

The deeper your gratitude runs, the stronger your drive becomes to lift others up. That fire inside you pushes past the walls that once kept you in the dark, and it compels you to pass on the same knowledge and grace you have received. This is what the New G Mentality is all about: a pay-it-forward spirit that sparks change not just in one life but across entire communities.

Always keep in mind that practicing gratitude is an ongoing journey, not a one-time event. It plays a crucial role in transitioning from hopelessness to hope and in creating a meaningful legacy. Many triggers might try to make you view your experiences through a negative lens that pushes you back into pain and unforgiveness. You'll face a choice: either dwell on your past that you cannot change or gather strength and perseverance to shape your new future. In these moments, it is your choice and responsibility to elevate yourself because no one can do it for you.

Embracing a new lifestyle means seeing every moment to breathe, grow, and transform as essential to cultivating gratitude and leading a more meaningful life. Daily inspiration arises from finding new chances to learn, adapt, and appreciate. Over time, you come to appreciate your life as an extraordinary journey, full of experiences that shape you into a unique person with special gifts to offer the world.

Your journey to the next level of success will be unique, shaped by **every single experience** and the resilience you've shown in overcoming seemingly impossible challenges. This fundamental grit will remain a vital force as you succeed and flourish, all while acknowledging your blessings and cultivating a Grateful Mentality.

Having faced many near-disaster scenarios in life, embracing a Grateful Mentality can boost your hope and motivate you to pursue greater goals. This is a pathway to foster freedom and motivate you to reach your full potential. It enables you to release burdens that hold you back and unlock your potential for growth. Beginning each day with a focus on gratitude can inspire your actions to achieve your goals and drive your progress.

Throughout this journey, your mind will begin to devise ways to support the transformation of gang and street life, thereby providing illumination for others to follow. You will then develop a sense of gratitude for the responsibility entrusted to you to uplift and safeguard your family and loved ones. With this perspective, you can reconstruct narratives and establish new connections, irrespective of your original path.

Remember, your choices are yours to make, and they truly shape your future. Be prepared for challenges ahead, as previous temptations will still call, and new opportunities will bring fresh temptations that may attract you. While friends and others can root for you and support your journey, it is up to you to always stay true to your own path. Be open to the kind and helpful people you encounter along the way, as they can help you grow. As you continue this exciting journey and start to see success, you'll find even more reasons to feel grateful and inspired.

Be always aware though. Wanting to change doesn't guarantee it will happen. Without shifting your perspective and the action behind it to create new lifestyle habits and add positive elements, the necessary changes will not be made. Life moves on, presenting many triggers and challenges that can hold you back. It's important to set aside intentional moments for reflection, which help you identify key moments in your life that keep you centered and grateful. Do your very best while working on your growth, and don't let setbacks distract you from your focus to move forward.

Think about this: if you're reading this book, you have made it through every good and bad situation in your past. Although the effects of some of the bad situations may still be present in your life, you've made it. Let that serve as a source of strength to boost your faith during the hardships you will experience in the future, knowing that you will overcome them as well. Even if you face losses and challenges, walk with confidence knowing there are still many things to be grateful for. Adopting this perspective is a catalyst for a significant shift in your mindset and future actions.

Understanding your life's journey can bring a sense of peace and gratitude. There's no need to wait for others to validate your success; it's all about setting goals and defining your own growth and achievements, because everyone's path to success is unique. Celebrate your wins, big or small, because that can really boost your outlook and inspire hope. However, don't make the mistake of thinking that you have arrived. The war still goes on.

As the saying goes, "setbacks are just a setup for your comeback." Practicing gratitude gently reminds you that you are capable to face any challenge and grow stronger each day. By taking ownership and sharing your talents, you not only uplift yourself but also inspire those around you.

Real Stories 4: Creating Life

Everybody already knew what I was capable of. Nobody questioned whether I was real or if I could handle what came with the streets. I proved that. I stood on business, faced pressure, and survived situations that would have broken most people. I earned my respect, and my name carried weight. But after a while, I had to ask myself a real question. Can I do something new?

Destruction came easy because I was trained to survive in chaos. Anybody can tear something down. But creating life, building something that lasts, and speaking hope into people who gave up on themselves takes a different kind of strength. That is real power.

I started realizing that the same energy I once used to hustle, defend, and fight could be flipped into building, teaching, and protecting. It stopped being about proving I could still be hard and became about proving I could be whole. Growth did not erase who I was. It expanded who I could become.

Now when I move, I think about what I am creating. Real power is not in how loud my name rings in the streets. It is in how deeply my impact lives in people. Anybody can take a life, but creating one, my own or someone else's, is where I want my legacy to be.

Chapter 5
Grace Mentality: It Doesn't Erase the Past;
It Elevates You Beyond It.

The Grace Mentality is the mindset that recognizes as long as a person has a heartbeat, there is an opportunity for redemption. The New G Mentality wouldn't exist without grace because it would mean that extraordinary change is impossible.

Grace declares that your past decisions are not final and serves as a reset button in every life. It is the ability to forgive yourself, extend mercy to others, and move forward without being trapped by yesterday's actions.

The Grace Mentality is powerful because it breaks cycles of shame, guilt, and judgment that keep people anchored to the past. Grace creates space for healing, growth, and rebuilding. It shifts the focus from punishment to possibility, from failure to future. Grace reminds us that you don't have to be perfect to start; you just need to be willing to overcome and take the next step.

The essence of the Grace Mentality is centered on freedom. It involves embracing the truth that you are more than your worst decisions and understanding that extending grace to others increases the likelihood of transformation. Grace is not a sign of weakness;

rather, it is a form of strength that heals, unites people, and opens doors for change.

Your experience is the 'realest' thing you'll ever encounter because you've lived through it. Both good experiences and hard times are real and unique to you. No one knows your experience better than you. Because of this, it's common to find ourselves focusing more on the memories of tough times rather than the good ones. Hard times feel different because they tend to bring more pain and can sometimes be overwhelming and heartbreaking, making us want to steer clear of them whenever we can.

The trauma that comes with surviving daily life is real. For instance, taking a significant loss can be extremely painful, especially because you don't have much to begin with. If that loss was a loved one and it was due to violence, it can add another layer of hurt and trauma. Many other feelings and thoughts also accompany such situations. With violence, there might be anger and hatred toward those responsible, often leading to a desire for revenge that can be hard to overcome.

That's why, as you grow in your New G journey, nurturing a Grace Mentality becomes truly important. This mindset allows you to adopt a positive perspective as you consider all sides of any problem or scenario. By considering different angles of a situation, you'll naturally see reasons to extend grace and forgiveness, even to those who might not seem to deserve it at first glance.

Maturing in this mindset promotes your development because it shifts your focus to trying to understand rather than being understood. Your feelings and thoughts are valid, and you are already clear about how you think and feel. What remains uncertain is the other side of the equation, where a person or situation presents a different perspective that you must understand to have the complete picture. Learning to understand the other side of a situation involves gaining insight into the feelings and thoughts of others, allowing for a more comprehensive and logical conclusion. This helps you consider multiple rational options instead of getting stuck with a single thought created only by the information in your head.

Understanding helps explain how life's experiences have caused harm to people and why they often act out a script that caused harm to others. This perspective can help you see someone not as an enemy, but as someone who has been hurt and truly needs compassion. By closely analyzing the situations, you can identify the root causes that have influenced your thoughts and those of others, revealing how these influences led to similar behavior patterns. Applying grace and forgiveness to these situations can mend deep wounds and create opportunities for positive connections.

Many elements of life can influence doing good, and it is impossible to list them all. However, some key principles from this book include seeing others not as enemies, honoring those who came before us, working toward a brighter future for the next generation, and regularly seeking ways to contribute positively to your environment are all ways to do good.

When you humanize people and do not see them as enemies, your focus shifts toward fostering unity with those who are like you, who share similar desires and, regrettably, often have similar experiences. Choosing to extend grace to others genuinely nurtures a sense of connection and understanding. It's like building a bridge that guides us through life's ups and downs, allowing us to learn and grow together. Just like a bridge shortens the distance between two places, bridges of grace allow us to collaborate and shorten the distance between where you stand today and the future you are building for tomorrow. When we take responsibility for creating a better future with those around us, we help lessen the struggles and painful cycles that many face, fostering a more compassionate and hopeful community.

Throughout this journey, you must be willing to put in effort to elevate your mind. Remember, this is something only you can begin and complete. Your journey is unique to you, and taking the first step is entirely in your hands. It is your duty to use your unique life and outlook to solve problems and challenges that lead you closer to solutions that can assist others in confronting similar life struggles. This is only possible through grace in action, which involves extending grace to those in need and accepting responsibility to use the grace you have received.

What happens if you choose not to extend grace? It's like taking medicine; results can vary. But one thing is clear: you will block your ability to reach higher levels beyond self-interest. Refusing to show grace and forgiveness keeps devastation and destruction at the center of your actions and thoughts, hindering growth and progress in your life and for those around you. The path of destruction is a heavy burden to bear. The strongholds on the former path do not lead to healing but perpetuate cycles of death, poverty, and imprisonment.

Practicing grace and allowing it to help you calm intense emotions are essential steps toward achieving peace. When you feel at peace, it becomes easier to understand what you genuinely want for your life to improve. If you truly think about it, peace is the main thing you are looking for. In all the money you try to get, the fun you have, and whatever you do, **peace is the ultimate outcome that you are seeking**. I could be wrong, but in life, I have found this to be true from the people I have had this conversation with.

This awareness gently reminds you to focus not just on others, but also on valuing your own feelings and dreams. It opens your eyes to the great potential within you, encouraging you to explore and embrace it. This realization expands your outlook, revealing that those around you may also not have realized their full potential. With grace, you understand you have been granted another opportunity to discover and pursue that potential.

Living by and through grace allows you to forgive someone or give them a pass, recognizing their humanity and the importance of the greater good. Grace helps you to choose to overlook their actions, understanding that they were acting out of a destructive script and have been blinded, just like many others.

Grace embodies the idea of seeing things from other perspectives. This requires a process to develop that skill. One way is the development of Higher–Order Thinking (HOT). HOT is elevating your perspective of the world. It's the ability to go beyond surface reactions and think critically in a way that fosters understanding, growth, and transformation, prompting you to consider why it happened, where it originated, and what you can do about it.

You begin to realize the pain that has shaped others, their struggles, and their own unfortunate life circumstances. That shift opens the door to grace, even when you've been hurt. Instead of staying stuck in anger or revenge, you choose to respond with wisdom, compassion, and a plan for change.

HOT is more than just knowing; it's how you turn knowledge into power. HOT utilizes skills such as critical analysis, problem-solving, and creativity to transcend mere memorization or reaction. It challenges you to connect concepts, evaluate situations, and make well-reasoned judgments that create new understanding. In the New G Mentality, HOT is what lets you step back, look at life from another person's perspective, and see the bigger picture. When things make you "hot" in life, HOT (Higher-order Thinking) follows these three steps:

1. See Beyond the Moment

> Step back and evaluate the situation. Ask why something occurred, connect the dots, and consider the larger picture, which includes the other person's point of view.

2. Think With Wisdom and Understanding

> Apply critical thinking and creativity to assess your choices. Seek solutions that promote peace, healing, and growth rather than repeating harmful cycles.

3. Choose to Transform

Make a decision that leads to new outcomes for you, your family, and your community. HOT thinking transforms pain into purpose and problems into opportunities.

When you practice HOT, you give yourself the power to rise above the first reaction and respond with intention. Remember, **extending grace doesn't excuse what happened; it transforms what happens next.** It allows you to choose peace, build bridges, and live a different way forward, modeling a path that brings healing to yourself, your family, and your community.

During your New G transformation, you may still feel the urge to act or retaliate. While it is important to acknowledge these feelings and thoughts as genuine, it is equally vital to challenge them to prevent acting impulsively. In reality, revenge is temporary and doesn't resolve the root issue. It's a trap that can pull you back to sabotage your growth.

By choosing grace over revenge, you immediately grow and release others from harm, while allowing them the chance to grow. You free yourself from the role of enforcer and trust that life will unfold as it should, even without retaliation. This creates a peaceful mental space and opens up opportunities for positive actions to enter your life.

Just as we discussed in the chapter on gratefulness, forgiveness is essential for extending grace. Grace and forgiveness are not only acts given to others, but they also serve as a powerful act of freedom for yourself. This form of forgiveness requires recognizing misplaced loyalty and situations where you have been misled and freeing yourself from the weight of walking in unfulfilled potential and the lies that once held you hostage. Forgiveness invites you to let go of burdens from circumstances beyond your control, enabling self-forgiveness for harmful choices, and living to break cycles of trauma that impact your life and community.

I must emphasize this again. Forgiving others isn't about excusing their actions, but about exploring the reasons behind what they did so we can respond with empathy and sometimes sympathy. Even when their choices are still wrong, understanding reminds us that everyone faces human struggles and desires.

Nobody, which includes everybody, is perfect, and everyone has made bad choices. We all, in some way, have contributed to pain and chaos. Forgiveness helps us let go of defining others by their worst moments and lightens the burden of resentment. If we continue to hold on tight to unforgiveness, we only create our own difficulties, blocking growth and keeping reconciliation out of reach.

A Grace Mentality is about forging a truce with yourself and others to collaborate and achieve higher goals. It acknowledges that meaningful change demands deliberate effort, without which nothing changes. These acts strengthen your character and help you see and experience life with strength and purpose.

Getting to this type of mindset and lifestyle doesn't happen by accident. You must make a conscious decision and put in the daily work to unlearn old habits that hinder your growth, kindness, compassion, and forgiveness. When you put in the work, don't expect anything in return from others because they might not notice your transformation and growth. The main thing is you notice it and trust the process. This requires a lot of effort, but consistent effort makes you stronger and will lead to a life that's deeper and more meaningful.

If you have been taught to survive by "any means necessary," shifting from a survival mindset to one rooted in trust and grace is required to thrive. You must begin with introspection to conduct an honest self-assessment, allowing you to recognize your flaws and see the common humanity in others. This isn't about self-criticism but about cultivating humility and laying a solid groundwork for growth.

Grace changes everything. It turns pain into purpose and struggle into strength. When you carry a Grace Mentality, you meet people where they are, whether tired, broken, or ready for a fresh start, and offer acceptance, love, and hope without judgment. You listen with compassion, look past faults, and open the chance to become a guiding light. This is transformation in action, where it is real, raw, and contagious, calling you to help others step boldly into new beginnings.

With your inspiration and support, people will be guided to become an essential part of the community and heal from past rejection, hurt, and trauma. Unmerited grace transforms lives so deeply that paying it forward becomes a necessity. Seeds of grace will continue to be sown and grow, fostering a culture where shared care and acceptance are the norm rather than the exception.

One last warning, though: don't be misled. By adopting a Grace Mentality, you gain a positive outlook and a different way to connect with people, but it doesn't prevent conflicts. Conflict will arise when you least expect it. It is inevitable. Although we usually perceive conflict as disagreements among people, it can also arise from external obstacles that hinder progress. All feelings of conflict are legitimate. However, the most significant conflicts often originate from internal mental, spiritual, and emotional barriers that limit growth and slow advancement.

Throughout the change process, it is common to have conflicts between your existing knowledge and new learning. These reflect two different aspects of your life. When these two aspects clash, and you feel that inner tension and conflict, don't paralyze your progress and go back to what you know. Taking a step forward in your new life and push past the pull that is trying to take you back to your old life.

So on the one hand, you have the comfort of familiarity, which involves doing what you have always done and trying to build something better with the same tools. These tools represent your past experiences, successes, failures, joys, and sorrows that form the foundation of who you are. They provide a sense of identity and stability, anchoring your worldview. The problem is these tools rarely build what you truly desire, and they conflict with your commitments to growth and learning, which are real and tangible.

On the other hand, as you change and face the challenge of the unknown, every new step is a step of faith, trusting that as you put in the work and gain new tools, you will build your life toward a place of peace and success. Every new piece of knowledge you acquire will elevate you beyond your past experiences, pushing you into the unknown and opening up new possibilities you never knew existed.

Applying grace to situations is one of those tools that can provide a fresh perspective on every aspect, including conflict. The new way of living will constantly reshape and improve you. This ever-changing outlook on life inspires you to step outside your comfort zone and rethink your assumptions about life. It's a journey of discovery and growth, where each new piece of knowledge or skill helps you better navigate life's ups and downs.

Your past does not define you! **Your ongoing growth seasoned with grace will define you**. In times of conflict and difficulty, remember that you are still learning and can grow beyond your previous limits. Accepting this duality allows you to appreciate the value of both stability and change. Resilience is developed by combining lessons and hardships from the past with the strength and purpose to face what lies ahead.

This method turns the conflict between existing knowledge and new learning into catalysts for growth, enabling you to become a more refined, capable, and graceful person. This grace sustains your progress and prevents complacency even amid chaos. It encourages you to view life's darker sides not as your full reality but as chances for growth and essential change.

If gangs have been your way of life, your past can often feel like a cycle of death rather than living. Your transformation can also come to feel like a death of sorts. You are dying to the bondage that was holding you back. However, you are not dying; you are growing into a New G and moving into a new life with the same familiar people, developing a greater purpose. So, you are not losing family; you are gaining life.

Cultivating a Grace Mentality can guide you and those you've shared your previous lifestyle with toward redemption. Grace will show you that your past is forgiven and empower you to choose a new future. By doing so, you can foster a community founded on redemption, where grace is seen as both a personal virtue and a collective value.

Nurturing a Grace Mentality is a journey that involves refining strength through discovery and empathy for transformation. This strength allows you to deliberately demonstrate kindness, understanding, and forgiveness toward yourself and others. As you adopt this mindset, your compassion deepens, drawing you closer to the world around you. Those who were once enemies will become allies in growing the New G Movement, a space where grace is both given and received, creating a powerful force for positive change and redemption.

Real Stories 5: The Day I Chose Growth

I remember the exact day I decided I was done. I was sitting in a cell staring at the ceiling, realizing I had spent years giving my best energy to destruction. Every move, choice, and fight was about survival, not living. I realized I had mastered how to hustle and make things happen in the middle of chaos, so I started asking myself, "What if I used that same drive to build something different?"

I couldn't answer that question at the time. I just started to do what was necessary, like reading stuff that could help me see different, listening to new things, and challenging my thinking. I began learning how to control my thoughts instead of letting them control me. I started practicing patience, even when everything in me wanted to rush. It was hard at first, and I don't even know how a lot of the change happened, but something shifted inside me. I was beginning to see life and people differently and grow into someone new.

I just started a process that helped me grow. I made it a point to stop living for the old life and started living to invest in myself and those who came from the same streets. Every day I make the same choices again to learn, to rise, and to keep becoming the person I was always meant to be.

Chapter 6
Giving Mentality: The Generosity Paradigm

The Giving Mentality is an anomaly, which means an uncommon way of living that deviates from the norm, breaking the common rule of self-interest and shining as a rare example of true generosity. It flips the idea that it's all about what you can get and challenges you to pour into others.

Giving isn't only about money. It's about investing time, energy, knowledge, and resources to uplift those around you. It flips the script on survival thinking and demonstrates that generosity multiplies where hoarding divides. Giving builds trust, strengthens relationships, and brings communities together.

Having a Giving Mentality essentially involves leaving a legacy that surpasses what you have taken and planting seeds that outlive you. Giving isn't a loss; it's an investment. It reflects leadership by recognizing that what you give today sets the foundation for tomorrow's freedom.

The Giving Mentality illuminates a paradox that the act of giving is also a form of receiving. When you give of yourself and your resources, you receive back meaning and purpose, along with many other benefits too numerous to mention. This mindset breaks the boundaries of fear, transforms lives, and shapes a world where compassion and interconnectedness are valued and supported. By adopting generosity, individuals become the seeds of positive change, leaving a lasting impact on the fabric of humanity.

Having a Giving Mentality involves moving from a self-centered focus to a desire to use your time, knowledge, resources, and efforts to support and uplift the broader community. It reflects the understanding that genuine growth and achievement come from sharing kindness, support, and resources with others. When you give, you become part of a community of people from diverse backgrounds united by a common good, breaking down boundaries and restoring dignity through the recognition of generosity's power.

Those who adopt the Giving Mentality are inspired to act and make a positive difference. It's not about having an abundance of resources, but rather about recognizing a need and finding ways to meet it with what you have. Giving becomes a way of life, a reflection of your heart and character. As you give, you don't just release something, you receive something greater in return. Each act of generosity enriches your life with knowledge, understanding, and purpose, helping you grow into a more compassionate and wiser person. It creates a cycle where the more you pour out, the more you are filled and enabled to keep giving and making a lasting impact.

You might think that if you have more resources, giving will be easier, but that's not always the case. Giving really depends on your heart and mindset, as well as your desire to contribute, which fuels your willingness to help. Remember, you always have something valuable to offer, no matter how small it may seem. This realization can lead to truly meaningful change; the most profound effect is on you, as it brings a sense of fulfillment.

If you've lived for twenty or more years, you've likely heard the saying: "It is better to give than to receive." If we are honest, we often feel it is better to receive than to give, especially because of the losses and hardships in life. Giving can be challenging when you're striving for more in life or believe you have nothing to offer. In such situations, it may seem irrational to use your limited resources and risk weakening your position. However, a Giving Mentality unlocks a generosity paradox that provides your soul with something money can't buy. It provides your life with faith that opens up new experiences and wealth that is beyond your earning power. Remember, your generosity is an investment to reap a harvest of meaningful impact throughout your life.

Giving is a multifaceted act of kindness that can be expressed in many ways. It's often viewed as a sacrifice, but for the New G, giving is always an investment. This kind of investment extends beyond just financial contributions. It also involves the value you bring and the unique gifts you offer to help others. The right investments will yield returns, even if they aren't immediate. Believe that contributing your time, thoughts, money, or efforts will generate opportunities for change that extend beyond your original action.

If you have taken the time in life to reflect on your actions, you probably noticed how your choices can have a significant impact on your outcomes. I recall times when I chased after a self-centered cause, thinking it was harmless, only to realize it caused pain to many people, including myself. My investment in the wrong things yielded unexpected and undesirable returns. However, these experiences taught me a valuable lesson, that what I invest in gives a return.

This led me to consider whether investing my time, knowledge, money, or efforts into positive pursuits would yield positive outcomes. By elevating my Giving Mentality, I realized that as I invested in good things, I began to yield positive results that brought benefits that exceeded my expectations. This is not an individual experience either. Many others with a sincere Giving Mentality have also achieved similar outcomes.

Adopting a Giving Mentality not only produces unexpected benefits but also generates a ripple effect that benefits others. Ultimately, shifting from selfishness to purposeful giving benefits you and demonstrates that genuine fulfillment stems from contributing to something greater than ourselves.

TIME

Dedicating time to help others is a way to show generosity. It brings deep personal rewards and increases your sense of purpose and fulfillment. Volunteering provides an opportunity to assist those in need. When you start volunteering, you experience immediate satisfaction through tangible results and fulfillment from aiding the well-being of others. It satisfies a natural desire to connect and support. Additionally, it builds stronger community ties and boosts your sense of belonging and purpose.

Volunteering offers numerous benefits, including the acquisition of new skills and experiences that are valuable in many aspects of life. Volunteering provides unique tasks and challenges that differ from everyday routines, offering opportunities to learn, grow, and lead. Whether you are enhancing communication, developing leadership, or understanding different lifestyles, these experiences can enrich you both personally and professionally. By stepping outside your comfort zone and trying new activities, you create transferable skills, which are opportunities for growth and development.

If you look beyond the personal growth, investing your time can also enhance relationships and social connections. By engaging with like-minded individuals who share your values, you have access to areas where you can grow and foster meaningful friendships. This creates a supportive network and an enriching environment that sparks a ripple effect of kindness and compassion. Observing such generosity can promote a more compassionate and supportive society for all.

KNOWLEDGE

Sharing knowledge and insights boosts collective wisdom and problem-solving. When experiences are shared, they contribute to a larger knowledge pool that everyone benefits from. This collaborative method appreciates diverse perspectives, fostering innovation and effective solutions. Through the exchange of knowledge, both organizations and individuals can make more informed decisions, drive progress, and achieve their goals more efficiently.

Sharing knowledge also promotes personal growth by pushing you to broaden your understanding, enabling you to contribute more effectively. It involves understanding different perspectives to expand your worldview. Through this process, you will learn to explain complex ideas, which helps to clarify your thoughts and deepen your understanding of the subject. This practice strengthens your knowledge while exposing you to new insights and viewpoints. Participating in idea sharing promotes ongoing learning and mental engagement, helping to keep your mind active and your skills sharp.

Sharing your thoughts and expertise openly fosters trust and collaboration, building goodwill and opening doors to partnerships. When people feel appreciated and supported, they are more likely to engage and reciprocate. Cultivating strong connections unlocks new opportunities for success and fulfillment.

Through knowledge sharing, you are fostering a culture of empowerment and capacity building, which equips you and others with the essential tools for driving growth and development. As your knowledge and skills grow, you'll be better prepared to seize new opportunities, making meaningful contributions to communities and vital stakeholder sectors that enhance entire systems and support a more capable and resilient society.

One example of sharing knowledge and strengthening systems occurred when I collaborated with a historically recognized nonprofit organization that was new to the field of justice-involved reentry. They had a decent plan for approaching reentry, but it lacked elements that would make them stand out. I was invited to share my knowledge early in their development.

Due to my lived experience and perspective, I was able to share insights and knowledge about the reentry process and the challenges faced by justice-impacted individuals. This motivated them to extend their efforts beyond programming, fostering a supportive environment that restored dignity and respect. This sharing of knowledge contributed significantly to the organization becoming one of the leading reentry groups in the city.

Sharing your experiential expertise and knowledge does more than offer ideas; it drives change. Your wisdom is priceless to those unfamiliar with your world. It serves as a key that helps others see differently and leverage their resources for meaningful impact. Your education is unique, and by sharing it, you become not just a contributor but the subject matter expert in a crucial process.

RESOURCES

Donating resources, such as money, often has a bad reputation because some fear it will be misused. Others think that limited funds only cover bills, leaving no extra money to give. However, in 2023, the Annual Report on Philanthropy estimated that about $557.16 billion was donated in the U.S. When giving financially, the focus should be on supporting worthwhile causes, such as organizations dedicated to redeveloping and empowering gangs, rather than emphasizing the negatives of giving.

Supporting and sustaining organizations benefits both the recipients and you, the giver. When an organization receives contributions, it has the advantage of addressing urgent needs, and you become a direct champion for their success, which also becomes your success.

Collective giving to the right causes grants access to vital resources for those in need. This immediate support significantly enhances the quality of life for individuals, families, and communities, enabling them to build a more stable future. People with the New G Mentality are encouraged to focus on finding ways to take responsibility and invest in addressing critical needs that matter to them.

Individual donor support enables programs to plan and implement their initiatives more effectively. This reduces dependence on uncertain grant funding, which often comes with restrictions and a competitive selection process. Consistent donor contributions enable organizations to respond quickly and effectively address emerging needs. This flexibility benefits participants by enhancing programs and offering support to help them move beyond their current situations and find chances for progressive growth.

Sustaining programs through your donations encourages a deeper sense of community ownership and engagement. You become part of a team or group dedicated to taking responsibility for a specific area to make the necessary changes. When you contribute financially, you deepen your commitment, making you more invested in the success and impact of those you serve.

This shared investment often leads to increased volunteer involvement, advocacy, and backing for the cause. By establishing a broad network of financial supporters, organizations can cultivate more resilient and dedicated community connections, providing a strong foundation for sustainable change and growth.

By embracing generosity with your resources, you become a key resource in enhancing lives and enabling those around you to function effectively without relying solely on external help. As a New G, your contribution helps sustain the movement to build a solid foundation for the long-term stability of important improvement plans. Additionally, your generosity provides personal fulfillment and purpose, knowing that you make a positive difference in bringing about lasting change.

EFFORT

The term "ministry" usually refers to serving or performing a role within religious, spiritual, or humanitarian contexts. However, it can also be used non-religiously to describe acts of personal service or love. For example, a ministry might be established to support specific groups, such as students, community members, or individuals with particular needs. In the case of the New G Mentality, it represents giving effort to serving and fulfilling a purpose rooted in a higher calling. This purpose isn't tied to a title or organization but centers on serving others as a form of giving.

Getting involved in ministry offers many benefits, beginning with a meaningful sense of purpose. It helps you connect your actions with your faith and core values, making your daily activities feel more connected to what you believe. This strengthens your sense of who you are and why you're here, as you see that your efforts contribute to a larger, more meaningful purpose. When you serve others, you nurture your spiritual and moral growth, which can fill your life with joy as you live out your faith in real, tangible ways.

Ministry often involves serving others, reflection, studying spiritual teachings, and engaging in prayer or meditation as you develop. These practices enhance your understanding of the Giving Mentality and deepen your consistent effort in ministry, fostering growth in wisdom, compassion, and spiritual maturity, while also bringing reciprocal blessings, helping you experience grace more profoundly in your life.

Another benefit of your efforts is that it frequently pushes you to take on leadership, organization, communication, and problem-solving roles. As you grow in these areas with a generous heart, you're sharpening your skills and boosting your confidence as a leader. As you excel with these abilities, they naturally transfer to other parts of your life, supporting your overall personal and professional development. Plus, ministry work gently pushes you out of your comfort zone, helping you develop resilience and adaptability along the way.

Dedicating yourself to serving others in ministry demonstrates compassion, selflessness, and a spirit of community. Promoting generosity within your community helps build a more caring and supportive environment. Generosity has a direct impact on individuals and communities, generating a ripple effect of service that leads to thriving.

GIVING MENTALITY CONCLUSION

The Giving Mentality stands as a beacon of light in a world that often seeks self-centered pursuits. The philosophy of giving transcends barriers, cultures, and socioeconomic divides, bringing people together through compassion and selflessness. Essentially, it reflects a genuine desire to help the well-being of others while also finding personal joy and fulfillment.

As a New G with a Giving Mentality, you are becoming an individual who naturally fosters a culture of generosity. Your thoughtful actions will lead others and set positive examples, creating a momentum that can move through entire communities. As this generous spirit takes hold, it strengthens social bonds and encourages a sense of connection among everyone. Ultimately, it becomes an effective way to bring about meaningful and lasting change.

Those who embrace this movement are genuinely passionate about advocating for positive changes in societal norms, policies, and practices. Their efforts not only provide immediate support but also help construct the foundation for lasting systemic improvements. When the New G is actively engaged, they create a meaningful legacy that can be passed down through generations.

Children will grow up seeing acts of kindness and giving as the norm, making it more likely they'll adopt these values and continue the tradition. By nurturing generosity, you're helping to shape a brighter future one step at a time.

Shifting your perspective to a Giving Mentality encourages valuing collective wealth alongside your personal gain. Supporting others in overcoming obstacles and reaching their goals empowers them to grow and thrive, fostering a cycle of mutual support. This also helps you elevate your efforts to the next level, and that level is leadership.

Real Stories 6: Becoming a Bridge

I grew up seeing how divided we were, not just between men and women but even among us as girls. At the time, I didn't understand that we were at odds for no real reason. We were fighting over attention, respect, or rumors that did not matter. Jealousy ran deep where love and support should have been. We tore each other down instead of lifting each other up, not realizing how much that kept all of us from growing.

As I got older, I started to see the pattern. The same pain that divided us as girls was keeping the whole community broken. I began listening more, talking less, and showing compassion instead of competition. That is when things started to change.

Sisterhood became more than just a word to me. It became my way forward. I learned that when women come together in truth and love, we create a strength that is not built on bitterness and a confidence that does not need comparison. I began to understand my purpose to be a bridge between men and women and to help reconnect sisters who forgot how to stand together. I have seen how powerful it is when we heal as sisters because when that happens, the whole community begins to rise.

Chapter 7
God Mentality: There Is Something Greater Than You

A God Mentality describes a mindset that influences our thoughts and actions because it emphasizes the existence of a divine power beyond ourselves. Adopting this viewpoint helps us recognize that everyone has inherent worth and a purpose greater than our own perceptions or assumptions.

Creation surrounds us and touches every aspect of our lives. When we observe all the things that have been made, we can recognize that each thing has a beginning, which can prompt us to consider a creator. The concept of the God Mentality signifies a profound concept of divine creation and the acknowledgment that human existence is purposeful rather than coincidental. This notion underscores the significance of life and fosters a connection with a divine presence that guides, supports, and nurtures us.

For this chapter, the God Mentality isn't linked to any specific religion, acknowledging that everyone is at different points in their spiritual journey. Still, I won't hesitate to share that I am a follower of Christ. My personal story and achievements are deeply rooted in how my faith experience has fueled my transformation, motivated new behaviors, and expanded my horizons. I believe that an individual who acknowledges God's existence and truth can effect change, thereby providing support to embrace an aspect of what it means to be a New G.

In the hardness of life, it can be nearly impossible to see that something greater sustains and nurtures the world and its people. Often, it feels the opposite, especially when personal desires go unfulfilled. You witness many evils that seem to be increasing, and nothing is being done to address them. This perspective, along with other challenges, may cause you to lose hope and let despair take root in your life. These elements and way of thinking start to form the foundation of your identity.

When hopelessness undermines your self-worth, it is essential to seek out counterinfluences that offer hope, support, and love. By doing so, you will have outlets that can help counteract negative thoughts. Without positive influences, you tend to resort to the first thing that appears to offer relief and momentary peace, even if you know it doesn't lead to genuine peace.

Overcoming the negative effects of personal experiences can be challenging because they are a part of what has shaped you. Even after your belief in God grows, moments of doubt or inner conflict will still arise because your new perspective will collide with your old experiences and held beliefs. Don't be discouraged by this.

Learning more about God's ways is not just about having faith. It is also about allowing the relationship to challenge and reshape old patterns of thinking. Through a deeper understanding of God, truth is revealed that dismantles lies, heals old wounds, and provides the courage to build a new foundation for life.

As the chaos of life starts to quiet down, allowing you to embrace peaceful reflection, you will begin to feel God's touch, providing comfort in difficult times and bringing clarity where things used to seem confusing. These are the moments that bring reassurance of hope, support, and love.

When I was young, I used to mock people who were in serious situations and turned to God, especially those who turned to God after going to jail. I was right there with many others saying, "You got that jailhouse religion." However, as I matured in my life and relationship with God, I realized that prison and other hard places are spaces where people can hear and accept God, because they offer the need for clarity amid chaos.

The challenge is that as you work toward developing a God Mentality, you often face opposition and will find it hard to maintain. This difficulty can arise in many ways. It can be other people's opinions of you, the conflict between your current actions and your desired lifestyle, or the simple desire to hold on to old things. During these times, you may want to follow God's guidance but still find yourself tempted to do things you know you shouldn't do. It is in these moments that God's voice becomes the loudest, using your conscience to warn you.

When your conscience speaks, you have the choice to either listen to it, which prevents you from doing the wrong action you're considering, or to ignore it and go ahead. In my past, I often dismissed my conscience by saying "F*** it!" and did what I knew was wrong. I found myself acting on my impulses without a second thought, having silenced my conscience and the feelings that were trying to stop me. They no longer mattered. The more comfortable I became ignoring my conscience, the easier it was to act against it.

I have come to understand that many people do or say things to go against their conscience warning them. I have also learned that not everyone involved in gangs is entirely opposed to God, even if it appears that way externally. They do possess a conscience, but it is often clouded by their circumstances and lifestyle.

There are times when a person wants to try to live for God, but they are involved in things that they cannot show softness or let God's ways override street codes. It is at this time that you must begin to reflect on the knowledge you are living by outside of God and ask yourself if this has provided the outcomes you are searching for. Once you consider this, you may start to see reasons to learn more about God and be more open to changing things that haven't produced the desired outcomes.

Having awareness of God will open your mind to see beyond your personal self-interest and see how you can interact with others and the world around you in a more connected way. This will help you to recognize the brokenness in the world presents a chance to turn to God for healing and strength. This awareness helps you to lead with empathy, compassion, and humility, because you recognize that everyone is imperfect yet inherently sacred and interconnected with all existence.

Starting your journey can feel like walking in blind faith, and in the beginning, it is, because you lack proof to guide you. You have to rely on faith and hope that your beliefs and actions are significant and destined. As you remain consistent in walking by faith, a shift will take place where you are no longer walking blind. You will be able to look back and see how God's presence has been with you all along, shaping a life full of purpose, depth, and significance. This transition takes you from blind faith to walking with evidence. The more evidence you gather, the more your faith and hope grow, as you recognize when and how God was revealed.

For those who may not adhere to or subscribe to traditional ideas of God, there is an acknowledgment of the universe's remarkable complexity and the beauty of creation. This perspective encourages reflecting on the idea that a greater force exists and that some mysteries are beyond human comprehension. Whether rooted in nature, human connections, or the search for truth and wisdom, it signifies an awareness of a higher intelligence. Such feelings often emerge during moments of reflection and discovery, especially when confronting your deepest fears, hopes, and vulnerabilities.

Whether you believe in God or not, cultivating an awareness of the divine will enrich your life experiences and deepen your understanding of how everything in existence is interconnected, aligning with a part of the New G Mentality. It promotes exploring questions about meaning, morality, and purpose, while encouraging reverence for the sanctity of life and the beauty of creation. Embracing this awareness allows skeptics and believers alike to find common ground in their shared quest for truth, wisdom, and wholeness amid a world full of mystery and wonder.

IDENTITY

The concept of shaping your identity was introduced earlier in the book. A primary goal of cultivating a God Mentality is to help people develop their sense of self by considering various factors that shape their identity and sense of belonging. Joining a gang usually provides a sense of community and acceptance. In the early development of their identity, it often becomes associated with loyalty, respect, and power as they seek validation and recognition within the gang. The code of the streets, style of dress, language, mentality, and other traits came together to shape who they were and their commitment to gang life.

This development was more than a simple process, as it reflected deep values that were used to define their identity. This became a source of pride and created a sense of belonging, while also serving as a way to stand up against perceived injustices and inequalities, as members worked toward finding their place in society.

Once a person becomes involved in gang activities and establishes their gang identity, participation in further illegal acts becomes central to their role. These acts are used to actually strengthen bonds of camaraderie, loyalty, and trust. Since most gang members develop their identity through participation in similar activities and experiences, connections are reinforced whenever they work together toward shared goals, whether it is crime or having fun, especially when there is potential for negative risks and consequences.

Despite the considerable risks, challenges, and negative consequences of gang involvement, the attraction remains strong because loyalty and trust are built and become a significant part of their identity. Their loyalty is second to none because those they run with are more than just people, they are family. The realization that this loyalty will result in them continually confronting the same negative outcomes never fully sinks in, because they're often loyal to a fault.

As people continue to live, there are times when they become more aware of the negative outcomes and begin to confront the realities and challenges of gang life, which may cause them to want to withdraw and pursue other paths of success and fulfillment. However, walking away from a gang identity can be a difficult mental and personal journey, because it requires redefining oneself outside the group, building new relationships, and finding supportive networks, which can feel unfamiliar and pose new challenges. There is also the fear of what others think and whether they would let you go.

The identity of gang members is not static but rather evolves over time in response to social, economic, and environmental changes, as well as maturation. This process of growth is similar for most people. As members age and their circumstances change, priorities also shift, leading to changes in desires for engagement and commitments to trouble. External pressures, such as risk of arrest, death, or losing a loved one, and internal pressures, such as personal experiences and health, can influence new survival strategies, thereby transforming their original identity.

As this shift occurs, the risk-versus-reward dynamic also changes. The reward that was once worth the risk no longer seems worth it. So, individuals often contemplate breaking free from the gang lifestyle. However, many internal challenges surface because it is breaking away from a core part of their identity.

The thought of abandoning everything they know and love feels disloyal, especially when it means leaving family. This is why one of the main principles of the New G is to redevelop gangs so that everyone can elevate at once, without having to turn their back on anyone. This way, everyone can be elevated, and the negative lifestyle and its consequences can disappear, not the people.

A good way to start addressing these identity challenges is by adopting a God Mentality. This perspective helps clarify your past and offers redemption, enabling you to make better decisions and take more informed actions as you start your new journey. The individual must see that their current approach cannot achieve what they truly want. Embracing the God-centered mentality can lead to a powerful, transformative experience that rises above the temporary and often harmful allure of old gang culture.

The appeal of power, respect, and promises is often brief and comes with high costs, including involvement in crime, violence, loss of personal freedom, and even death. In contrast, a connection with God offers true empowerment, achieved not through violence or intimidation, but through love, compassion, and grace. Living by this principle requires strength, but when you genuinely care about those around you, this should be your heart's desire. Such empowerment enables individuals to make positive contributions to their lives, communities, and society.

The current gang culture offers a significant sense of belonging and acceptance. It is crucial to recognize this, as the familial aspect is frequently overlooked. If they are required to sever ties with their familial relationships and establish new ones, they might feel as though they are abandoning their loved ones in pursuit of other groups. This disconnection may hinder their ability to adapt to new relationships, fostering a persistent fear of abandonment.

I'll use followers of Christ as an example of family. We are called a body of believers, and the Bible teaches that we are not like family, but we are family, an identity we should embody in our lives.

There's much growth needed in this area, as believers come from diverse backgrounds and perspectives, but you get the example.

As we come to terms with the fact that we are not like family, but are family, how would it look if we told people they need to abandon their current family to follow Christ? That doesn't make sense. The Bible does mention leaving old things behind (Philippians 3:13; 2 Corinthians 5:17-18), but abandoning loved ones is not the intended meaning behind these or any other verses. There are other verses that prioritize God first (Matthew 10:37-39; Mark 10:28-30), so if we tell people that the only way to follow Christ is to leave their family, that wouldn't make sense. So, telling a gang member that disconnecting from their gang family is the only way to improve their life breeds instability, shows no respect for family bonds, and overlooks the chance to elevate the entire family relationship to a higher good.

The God Mentality seeks to cultivate a culture rooted in genuine love, acceptance, and purpose. Just as gangs and followers of Christ thrive in family-like structures, no one is required to leave their circle or community in order to grow. Choosing to leave is still an option and a personal decision, but growth does not have to mean separation.

The offer is to create space for people to explore their identity through a higher purpose and a deeper understanding of their true worth, while staying connected and uplifting the same circles that have remained constant through tough times. Strengthening those bonds and nurturing growth within their relationships is essential for the New G's rise, elevating their life and becoming a positive force for others.

Discovering and nurturing your identity in God involves viewing yourself as a child of the Creator, who created you with unique gifts, talents, and purpose. This understanding boosts your confidence and sense of worth, driven by the belief that something greater within you elevates your value, an essential aspect of personal growth. Conversely, gang identity often centers around loyalty, opportunity, fear, intimidation, and conformity, which suppress individuality and personal expression. As people adopt a God Mentality, they uncover their true selves and gain the strength to forge a new identity while cherishing their foundational beliefs.

When you develop a God Mentality, you reshape your identity and adopt a new way of living. However, just because you become new doesn't mean you are better than others. It means recognizing that your life has greater value, and that you've improved beyond your previous state, and the activities you once engaged in fell short of your true potential.

Being involved with gangs doesn't limit your life to just engaging in criminal activities and the lifestyle you're used to. By living this way your mindset is restricted to a lower order of thinking. Living as a New G encourages you to elevate honesty, integrity, and compassion, which lead to higher levels of maturity. These values serve as a moral compass and may be contrary to your current view of building your life. However, when your new values guide you in making decisions and treating everyone with respect and dignity, including those who are different from you, areas of life that were once closed off due to a limited perspective will begin to open.

The core of developing a God Mentality is to support, encourage, and uplift your neighbors within your larger community. Gang relationships can shift from being volatile to being rooted in love, trust, and mutual respect. This approach fosters a desire for fellow gang members to pursue similar positive paths.

DEDICATION TO A GOD MENTALITY

Recognizing God's existence is a first step in cultivating a God Mentality. A crucial step for the New G is to build on this understanding on a daily basis. This involves a lifestyle and mindset change to become more mindful of how you interact with God and others. Your actions will serve as an example of areas where you need clearer direction, prompting you to seek God's guidance. As you elevate yourself, you will seek out coaches and mentors who can help you grow on your new journey to unlock your potential.

Knowing God and building on all the ways of a New G provides alternatives to the destructive and hopeless cycles of the current gang culture. By connecting to your new identity and purpose, you begin to shape brighter futures for yourself and those around you while living authentically and making positive contributions to life. Tapping into the God Mentality illuminates the illusions of independent control, helplessness, and self-sufficiency, guiding you toward steps in faith, progressive growth, critical thinking, and collaboration.

Adopting a God Mentality expands your understanding and perception of life, fostering convictions to overcome barriers and achieve breakthroughs. As you gain new experiences, you elevate beyond your previous efforts and choices that once caused despair. You realize you were never too deep on the wrong path to change, and by grace, you can let go of the past and build a new life. Mistakes and bad decisions will happen, but grace is always available to help you recognize and overcome them, enabling you to make the necessary changes and embrace new experiences.

Throughout my transformation as a follower of Christ, my life was still marked by bad choices and mistakes. There were things I thought I had moved on from in my life, only to find that old thinking resurfaced when I was put in certain situations. This was because my past lifestyle habits and the hardships I endured were real and a part of my subconscious thinking. Walking by faith has taught me that my journey is not about being perfect, but about applying grace to my mistakes and bad decisions, giving me time to understand God's ways and learn new lessons that help me overcome the challenges of early life. The God Mentality challenged me to make life changes that helped me overcome bad choices and greatly improved my way of living.

It takes time to grow a new lifestyle. I was twenty-two years old when I began to change my life, and it didn't start as fast as I would have liked. As I remained committed to growing, I decided to dedicate the next twenty-two years to discovering whether a God Mentality could make a difference. I committed to giving myself the same amount of time doing things that could help me be better as I did for things that might lead me to death.

Initially, the promises of God and this new lifestyle didn't seem logical to me, because there were so many things that were contrary to the way I lived my life, but I remained committed. When things didn't make sense, I relied on faith to see what would happen if I just kept moving forward. When faced with doing something new, I asked myself, "Will this hurt me or help me? If it isn't going to hurt me, and could possibly help me, what do I have to lose?" I would also test God by taking a scripture that contained a promise from God and would think to myself, "If I follow Your Word and it doesn't work out, then You cannot be true." Through grace and mercy, God gave me the time to learn and showed me that the promises were true.

I came across a Bible verse that said, "Taste and see that the Lord is good" (Psalm 34:8). I could relate to this verse because I know what it is like to taste food and see how good it is. I could rely on another person's opinion on what something tastes like, but it isn't the same. I can only truly understand what it's like by tasting it myself. That was the same with the Bible. I could listen to the opinions of others, or I could study for myself and find the truth. In testing God's Word, I realized it was way better than my own ways. However, this didn't mean it wasn't difficult to let go of my old ways of thinking and try something new. I enjoyed some of my old habits, but they limited my access to life.

I realized that my fear of letting go of old habits stemmed from the belief that I needed them to survive in the future. Much of my thinking was based on all I knew, and I believed some habits were necessary to get through life. However, this limited mindset prevented me from trusting God fully.

My distress influenced how I approached my daily walk with God, often causing me to act out of fear and despair, which kept me holding on to old thought patterns to shape my future. As a result, I would miss out on the present opportunity to build my life, because my worry and focus were on how I would live tomorrow.

When I realized I couldn't control tomorrow and learned to let go, I started to see how God provided so much that I could learn today, encouraging me to trust Him. I also understood that He was shaping me for my future. It all began with appreciating today, every day, and looking forward to each new day as an opportunity to learn and see what God can do.

I share this because adopting a God Mentality will change how you operate daily. Without change, nothing changes, and true change begins with you. When you change, your environment shifts even if your surroundings and circumstances remain the same. When you transform, better outcomes can appear much sooner than expected.

Although I committed twenty-two years to seeing if things would turn out differently, real progress happened sooner than I expected, clearly showing me that God's way is better. Most of my delay in experiencing God's blessings was due to the time it took for my actions and mindset to catch up.

My mind had to realize that the presence of pain sometimes propels us toward a greater purpose and shouldn't be avoided. Hardship not only refines our character but also opens our eyes to the struggles of others, awakening compassion and a drive to serve.

These moments of difficulty become a catalyst for self-discovery, guiding you toward your passions and the values that anchor you. When you embrace the full range of human emotion, including pain, you gain the ability to live authentically, turn trials into strength, and inspire transformation in those around you. This shift enables you to elevate your communities, foster deeper connections, and become an agent of change, ultimately making the world a better place because you chose to grow through what tried to break you.

Here's the good news: pain and suffering aren't the only parts of your journey. As you make choices along your path to transform, you'll begin to see things in a new light. Even when challenges come, you'll find yourself able to handle them with a fresh perspective and overcome them. Over time, you'll also notice an increase in joy, peace, and fulfillment.

As your outlook changes, gratitude will become more instinctive, and hope will start to replace despair. The negative thoughts that previously weighed on you will be replaced with more uplifting and empowering ones, causing your emotions to shift toward love, life, and a sense of freedom. With each step you take, life will take on more significance, allowing you to create positive memories and experiences that support your growth and remind you of why this journey is worthwhile.

Given that your growth may surpass the limits of your immediate local community, it's essential to embrace all aspects of development and expand your understanding beyond your current beliefs to fulfill a greater purpose. You were created for more, and now it's time to become the new version of yourself; the New G you were made to be. As you develop, you must trust the process of growth and get ready to participate in opportunities that were previously unavailable to you. If you stay ready, you don't have to get ready.

Walking with a mindset that honors God aligns you with the Creator, helping you to create new systems that break harmful cycles and support people in overcoming ongoing destruction and despair. This path will bring you new experiences that reveal your own redemption and clarify ways to restore others.

Through God's grace and mercy, you can leave behind past mistakes and decisions, embrace a new way of living, and strive toward a brighter future. You will realize that reconciliation provides more freedom than seeking retribution, which only leads to your demise.

Ultimately, knowing God and finding your true identity in Him opens the door to real freedom and peace. While gangs might seem to offer freedom through rebellion and defiance, this kind of freedom is often fleeting and doesn't heal the inner hurts and struggles we face. It's just an illusion, leading to wasted time, difficulties, more pain, and feelings of hopelessness. On the other hand, the freedom you discover through a relationship with God is authentic and transformative, freeing you from blame, shame, and remorse, and enabling you to live a life filled with purpose, joy, and fulfillment.

As you embrace God's direction in life, you'll connect with others who share similar experiences. In these moments, relationships are formed that provide comfort and support, turning what was once a lonely struggle into a shared journey. When you take these moments to extend God's everlasting comfort, whether through listening or compassion, you offer solace to fellow travelers. In return, there will be times when this same comfort is offered to you. This reflects the New G investment in growth rather than demise.

Real Stories 7: From Survival to Service

I survived things that should have taken me out. I faced bullets, time behind bars, and betrayal from people I trusted. For a long time, I thought being the hardest in the hood was the goal, but I have come to understand it was just how my life began.

I started to see that the way I was surviving was without purpose and empty. As I started to grow, I realized my story was never just for me. It was meant to plant something in others.

I was blessed to be able to start speaking at schools, sitting with young fathers, and returning to the same neighborhoods where I once caused pain. People ask me why I go back, and I tell them that I never left. I just found a new purpose to be someone who carries light into the places that have been forgotten.

Service became my way of giving back what life tried to take from me. I no longer see survival as enough. Real living begins when I use what I have been through to help others rise too.

Chapter 8

The New G Mentality: You are the Movement

Having a New G Mentality means choosing transformation instead of demise, purpose over mere survival, and legacy over harmful cycles. It's a conscious choice to channel loyalty, discipline, resilience, and leadership that is rooted in gang culture and redirect it toward creating families, businesses, and communities. This mentality isn't about abandoning where you come from and your gang family. It's about redeveloping the structure to achieve better outcomes. The New G Mentality encourages you to realize that the same determination that helped you use risky activities to get through tough times is your stepping stone for achieving greater success.

The New G Mentality explains how to go from the block to the blueprint and is foundational for the New G Movement. The movement embodies Growth to keep learning, Grit to keep pushing, Gratitude to stay grounded, Grace to rise after mistakes, Giving to lift others along the way, and all on a foundation of God to create some Good Trouble. Having a New G Mentality means living with the conviction that change is possible, that your life carries value, and that your impact can ripple far beyond the block. It is more than just a mindset; **it activates the movement** within us all to declare that who you are becoming is greater than your past experiences.

The New G can either remain a myth or rise as a movement; the choice rests with you and your circle. Your gang, your crew, and your community have the power to be the driving force that shapes what comes next. Every day, you will decide which version of yourself will grow stronger. Feed fear, division, and the old way of thinking, and the New G remains a myth. Feed vision, discipline, and purpose, and the movement ignites.

Choose to feed the future and be the spark that transforms your circle into a force for good. Challenge each other to grow, to heal, and to build something that outlasts the pain and chaos of the past. Remember, what you feed will lead, so choose to feed the movement.

Complaints often arise that no one is stepping in or stepping up to help or make changes in communities, which has truth to it. These calls for help to end the cycle of poverty, incarceration, and death often lack the support of people and laws needed to create real change. So, instead of just pointing out the lack of support for change, perhaps it should be a call for people to come together and think about the impact they can make by investing collectively in transformation.

The core idea of the New G Mentality is to bring together individuals, organizations, companies, governments, educational systems, healthcare systems, and similar entities to collaborate on improving their higher-order thinking skills, promoting stability, and cultivating leaders who uplift communities. Offering opportunities for personal and community growth can generate a ripple effect, raising living standards and building on the foundation laid by many individuals and organizations for change.

People involved in gangs and living in underserved communities often seek better lives amid economic hardships that cause desperation. The widespread desire for a better life drives individuals to pursue different opportunities within their environments. Gangs provide a sense of identity and purpose through their organized structures and familial bonds. Therefore, the focus should not be on dismantling these structures but on expanding options for wealth, health, and community development.

The key to breaking these cycles is not about fixing long-standing broken systems, but about creating new and improved opportunities to redevelop gangs. Over time, more gang members will develop and adapt to these new opportunities, helping them reshape their systems toward positive outcomes. History shows that repeatedly using the same survival tactics results in stagnant and harmful cycles. Therefore, the fight for change should start from within and motivate others on the outside to join in.

The New G Mentality aims to inspire a movement that demonstrates how gangs can leverage their existing infrastructure to promote development, generating opportunities for positive change. This strategy enables breaking cycles of violence and incarceration, diminishing the loss of loved ones, and enhancing community well-being. Uniting individuals establishes the foundation for wealth and an improved quality of life.

Now is the time for individuals to rise up and embody the change they want to see. This movement is more than just a passing trend; it's vital for progress toward a better life. Sustainable change must come from within communities, led by those most familiar with the issues and capable of guiding the desired transformation. This process won't happen overnight, and we should allocate the same amount of time it took to develop the gang culture over the past fifty years.

Numerous individuals and organizations have dedicated years to addressing the issues that plague our communities. The New G Movement does not seek to replace their efforts but instead provides a collaborative approach to building an infrastructure that unites us in progress. It is imperative that we all commit to fostering positive change and developing new opportunities to address the social determinants of health impacting underserved communities.

The development of systems and frameworks demands a collective effort to ensure the benefit of all stakeholders. Expanding opportunities for gang members is crucial in addressing societal challenges. This strategy involves dismantling notions of competition and fostering unity among gangs to facilitate meaningful change. The New G Mentality underscores the importance of growth and development for marginalized individuals, with all participants recognizing their vital and indispensable roles in this movement.

Picture a city where street corners symbolize opportunity rather than danger. Groups once focused solely on defending territory now foster community pride by organizing clean-ups, mentoring youth, and supporting small businesses. Streets previously illuminated by memorial candles are now covered with murals that depict stories of resilience and renewal. Instead of responding to violence, residents come together to celebrate achievements, such as graduations, employment, and ribbon-cutting ceremonies. Police officers and outreach workers work side by side, emphasizing prevention rather than crisis management. Trust is gradually restored through a steady presence and shared objectives, fostering a safer and more connected community.

Schools transform into avenues of opportunity instead of pathways to incarceration. Redeveloped gangs motivate their younger members to stay in school, earn credentials, learn trades, or start businesses. Older members serve as role models, emphasizing mediation over retaliation, entrepreneurship above negative pursuits, and service over chaos. As a result, incarceration rates decrease, community health improves, and violence declines, freeing up millions of public funds to be redirected into parks, training centers, and overall health initiatives.

The perception of gangs shifts nationwide from problematic to collaborative, from dangerous threats to thriving networks. The New G Movement embodies the possibility of change, creating not only safer communities but also stronger, more united ones where excellence becomes the norm.

The movement starts now and begins with you! Start to collaborate with others to create a better life that everyone desires and deserves. For this movement to be sustainable, adopt new strategies, open fresh opportunities, and establish innovative ways of living to pass along to others and future generations. Supporting a movement driven by community involvement and the emergence of transformative leaders is essential to bringing this vision to reality. NOW THAT'S GANGSTA!

www.ingramcontent.com/pod-product-compliance
Lightning Source LLC
LaVergne TN
LVHW051128080426
835510LV00018B/2300